Thriving Through Life's Transitions

PATRICIA A. BELL

Qui 2 Life Publishing
34 Shining Willow Way
LaPlata, MD 20646
www.qui2life.com
1 (301) 710-5219

Print ISBN: 979-8-9869513-3-1

eBook ISBN: 979-8-9869513-2-4

Library of Congress Cataloging-in-Publication

Author Name: Patricia A. Bell

Title: Thriving Through Life's Transitions

Edited by: Kyana Robinson and T. Lynn Tate

Cover Design by: Olayemi Bolaji

Scriptures taken from Holy Bible, King James, Message, NLT, and NIV versions at Biblegateway.com, Public Domain.

Dedication

I dedicate this book to my Lord and Savior, Jesus Christ, and the precious Holy Spirit, who brought all things back to my memory to write this book.

In memory of my parents, Mary Norman and Floyd Philip Gray, who adopted and raised me to be the Woman of God, I am today. They taught me to have faith in God. My mother left me with this saying, "Only the Strong Survive."

I also want to dedicate this book to those who have been hurt, brokenhearted, distressed, divorced, raped, homeless, lost loved ones, and even lost their faith in God. Remember that with God, all things are possible to them that believe.

Acknowledgments

First, I want to acknowledge God, the Lord of my life, who led me by the Holy Spirit to write this book.

To my daughter, Teneisha, thank you for inspiring me to tell the world my story. You motivated me to continue to write when I felt like giving up.

Special appreciation to Chandler Bolt, Self-Publishing School, and his staff for helping me get started with the mindmap and outline for my story. Thank you, Ellaine Kiel, for encouraging, inspiring, and praying with me as I went through the course in detail and with illustrations. I still hear you affirming, "Patricia, you will write and finish your book."

To my publisher and writing coach, T. Lynn Tate, I am thankful to you for all your time, support, inspiration, encouragement, and prayers. I am grateful for the many coaching sessions to help me with editing, writing, and listening to the Lord for downloads when I got stuck. Thank you for constantly reminding me that with Yahweh, I got this!

To Mother Annie Hungerford and Deaconess Martha Forston, I am grateful for your prayers and encouragement to share my story.

A Note for You

Dear Reader,

In life, we all face transitions. The new job, new baby, new house, new friends, and relationships are all transitions that promote joy and happiness. However, some transitions can invoke fear, sadness, anxiety, and depression.

This book is for those who have been through the fire of transition and left feeling heartbroken, wondering if and how they would ever recover. If that's you, I want to encourage you through my life's journey and the steps God gave me to thrive despite life's tests.

As you read, I pray that you will be inspired and encouraged to keep pressing forward and that you'll receive inner healing, restoration, and a renewed mind through a stronger relationship with God the Father through Jesus Christ.

Love, Patricia A. Bell

Chapter One

On May 7, 1949, I was born Carolyn Rebecca Thompson in a hospital outside Philadelphia, Pennsylvania. The details surrounding my birth are vague. However, I know that two of my biological cousins, Bill and Mary, and a nurse came to the hospital to take me to Covington, Virginia, with them. Mary and her husband, Floyd, adopted me and raised me with their eight-year-old biological daughter, Maggie.

We lived on Elk Street in Covington in a two-story white traditional house with green trimmings on an acre of land. A white fence enclosed our front yard and rose bushes and flowers lined the entrance of the front yard. To the side of the house was a clothesline where we hung our clothes to dry by the fresh breeze of the blowing wind. Two brick steps led the way up to our front porch and door. Most visitors to our home entered through the back door because we rarely unlocked and opened the front door.

My parents raised pigs in the nearby town of Wrightsville, Virginia. It was a small rural town with a church, a hotel, and two gas stations. During the summer months, my parents would slaughter the pigs and give away sausage, bacon, and pork chops. My parents also raised chickens in our backyard. On any given day, they would catch chickens, tie them on the clothesline by their feet and cut their heads off. Then my mother took them into the kitchen to wash and scrap the feathers off with a sharp knife. After watching all of that, I barely wanted to eat it.

My mother was a housewife, a cook, and a beautician. She did most of the women's hair in our neighborhood. The beauty shop was in a blue and beige brick building behind our house. Her beauty shop was full of flowers, and the scent of jasmine always filled the air. My mother would generously give her customers stems of flowers upon their request.

The shop area had a hair dryer, a wash bowl, and a styling station with a small cabinet above the hot stove. In addition, there was a recreation area in the room next to the shop. It was spacious, with a clothes dryer, a couch, a piano, and a record player. My friends and I often played games and practiced piano and dance routines in that room. My family also used this area to entertain and have parties.

My mother was a great cook, and I loved being in the kitchen with her. She taught me how to cook some of the most delicious meals. She also taught me how to bake various cakes and pies. One of my favorite dishes was Mother's fried chicken. The smell of that crisp and juicy goodness made my mouth water. Then she'd make hot yeast rolls to go with it, and the dance the aromas did together smelled like heaven.

While Mother cooked, I talked up a storm. Sometimes I talked so much that Mother would get distracted and forget to add some of her key ingredients. I must admit this happened a lot.

She often said, "Trisha, you sure have a lot of energy."

After a while, Mother realized she had to find ways to help me release some of my hyperness, as she called it. So, she strategically enrolled me in various lessons such as dance, piano, singing, and sewing. She also registered me as a Brownie in the Girls Scouts.

I loved being a Brownie. Our uniforms were brown. Of course, we participated in the annual cookie sale. Back then, cookies were only 35 cents a box. But that wasn't the most memorable thing about the Brownies for me. What I remember most was at the end of each meeting, we stood in a circle with our arms crossed, holding the hands of the girls next to us, giving a light squeeze to symbolize our friendship.

One summer, when I was a little older, I joined the regular Girl Scouts. Our uniforms were green. I went on several Girl Scouts' camping trips. I stayed a week at a time at different campsites where we slept outside in tents. Being mischievous, I would knock down the tents or spray bug spray in the other girls' tents at night, causing everyone to stand outside until the fumes were out of the tent. Naturally, this made everyone upset.

Occasionally, we stayed in this creepy white house on the grounds. In the spooky house, I would run around with a sheet on my head and scare the girls. Then I would run outside behind them, quickly removing the sheet before we all came together for a nightly count.

I'd ask my friends, "Who do you all think that was?"

I chuckled on the inside at their reactions. But, of course, they never figured out that I was doing the scaring.

Mother's plan worked. Not only did I have activities to keep me busy, but I gained new friends in the process. We didn't do much together, with Maggie being much older than me. She had her friends in her age group, and I had mine.

I attended Watson High School, which was an all-black school. Even though it was called a high school, the grade levels spanned from first through twelfth grade. The student body was about 405 students and was divided among fifteen teachers. I had the greatest teachers on Earth at that school. They instilled in me the priceless gift of strength and courage to face the future with knowledge and a high standard of morals.

Since the school was rather far from my house, my best friend, Elizabeth, and I were driven to school each day. Our fathers would alternate taking us, and when they couldn't, we would take a taxi. Because of this, other kids viewed us as privileged.

Back then, railroad tracks divided our neighborhoods. The kids that lived close to the school didn't like the kids from my side of the track. Our side of the tracks was considered the "other side" of the tracks. They would tease us and make us feel it was a bad thing that we were privileged.

Naturally, the teasing didn't help my disposition. During class, I was shy and would not answer when the teacher called on me. Instead, I would write a note and have my friend Elizabeth read it. I felt that anything I said was wrong and that no one wanted to hear what I had to say anyway. So, I would not say anything at all.

Around the age of seven, my adoption was finalized, and my name was legally changed to Patricia Ann Gray. I know my birth name was Carolyn, but I don't remember being called by that name as a child. When I was little, Maggie had so many nicknames for me that it took me a while to learn my real name. The first name she called me was Abbey. Then she started calling me Pattycakes. Finally, she settled on calling me Trisha, and so did everyone else.

Although I had been with my parents and Maggie my whole life, finding out I was adopted and that my name had been changed invoked a range of feelings. I felt angry and sad, but most of all, rejected and abandoned. I was hurt to the bone and cried from the shock and devastation. Since I had already silenced my voice at school, I now felt my voice didn't matter at home, either. So, from that day until I was in the 8th grade, I refused to speak a word and only conducted my life through written notes.

It would not be until later that I realized my adoption was a blessing in disguise.

Around the age of thirteen, I learned I had one biological brother and two biological sisters living in Gordonsville, Virginia, with my birth mother. The most hurtful part was realizing that I was not the youngest. Knowing that Esther, my younger sister, got to grow up with my mom further fueled my feelings of rejection and abandonment.

I often wondered and cried, "Why me? Why was I the one she gave up? What did I do to make her give me away? Where's my father? Does he even know I exist? Why did he let this happen?"

I still don't have the answers to those questions. The mystery of my father turned out to be a well-kept family secret, even to this day. I have two birth certificates, and neither shed light on my biological father's identity. I could have passed my father on the street and never even known it was him.

Adding to the stress of my home life were the bullies at the school. They took full advantage of my timidness and low self-esteem until I had enough. This one girl just would not lay off of me. She constantly taunted and teased me every day. Well, one day, I snapped, and I picked up a brick and chased her all the way to her house. When we reached her yard, her father was standing in front of the house. She ran behind him for protection.

I yelled, "She is always bullying me at school, and I want her to stop! If she doesn't, I'm going to knock her upside the head."

I think she got the message because she did not bother me anymore. But that wasn't the only thing that changed. After that day, my voice began to rise within me and busted out. I went from not talking at all to talking too much. I mean, I had a lot of years to make up for and a lot of thoughts and opinions to share.

I would talk during class and disrupt the lessons. Then, my teacher would make me sit in the hallway for everyone to see that I had been put out of class. It was embarrassing. Aunt Tina, who worked as a secretary at the school, would call my mother and tell her what had happened. When I got home, my mother would punish me and assign me more chores around the house.

I'm not sure if it was my antics, or simply my mother being overprotective, but my mother became very strict and kept track of my every move. She even became a cook in my school's cafeteria to keep a close eye on me. News of my misbehavior in class traveled like lightning with her on the school's premises. Although she didn't work there long, she was there long enough to get to know all my teachers very well.

A shift took place once I started speaking again, and life showed some promise. I became active in extracurricular activities at school. I joined the pom-pom squad, played on the basketball team, and even became a cheerleader. As a cheerleader, I traveled with the boys' basketball and football teams out of town on many occasions.

Surprisingly, my eagle-eyed mother did not accompany me on these trips, which was interesting because she didn't let me go anywhere without a chaperone. She wanted to know everything I was doing and who I was doing it with. At times, it felt like I was on lockdown.

Every Sunday, we went to church and Sunday school. This was my first line of defense for the upcoming week. If I did not attend Sunday school or church on Sunday, I was not allowed to do any other activities during the week. I sang in the junior choir, and while I didn't quite understand the meaning of baptism, a few of my friends and I accepted Christ as our Savior and got baptized at the tender age of 13. All I knew was that being baptized meant I could take communion in church like everyone else and not feel left out.

On youth Sunday at our Baptist Church, I was appointed to read the scripture. Unfortunately, when the time came for me to read, I would always get stage fright and freeze up like a deer in headlights.

Sitting in the congregation, my mother would yell, "Read, Trisha!"

It was so embarrassing, but it snapped me out of my frozen state. I'd read the Word of God and hurry out of the pulpit. What I didn't know then was that my mother was grooming and preparing me for the calling that was on my life.

When I was about fourteen, my parents adopted my little brother, Joshua. He was an infant, and I was responsible for helping my mom care for him. Daily, while my mother worked in the salon, I had to bathe, dress, and feed him. In addition to being a part-time nanny, I had to cook, clean the house, and wash and hang up the clothes, all while going to school and keeping up with my schoolwork and activities. Maggie was an adult and believed she was too old to do household chores.

There was no time for me to play and go out with my friends. If my friends came by to visit me, my mother would put them to work too. They would help me hang the clothes on the line and sometimes run errands to the store to get what my mother needed. There was always something that needed to be done.

I believe Mother kept me busy to stop my mind's idle thoughts about being adopted. However, she never told me why I was adopted or who my father was or might have been. Sadly, I don't recall ever getting up the nerve to ask her about it either.

After I turned fifteen, my biological mother passed away. Since she was my adopted mother's cousin, we attended her funeral. The best way to describe how I felt that day was numb. This was the first time I saw my birth mother, and she was lying in a casket. It was also the first time I would see my biological siblings. It was a lot to take in at that moment, and I was confused and unsure of how to feel.

I had two families, and I felt like a misfit in both. I had no relationship with my siblings, and at the time, I wasn't sure if I even wanted one. Even though my adopted family did their best to help me feel loved and accepted, the fact that I was adopted weighed on me mentally.

After my biological mother passed, my siblings stayed

with her sister, Dot. The following summer of 1963, my mother sent me and Maggie to spend our summer break with Aunt Dot and my siblings in Gordonsville, VA. It was a small town with a population of about 2,000 people, and it was pretty different from my life in Covington. We called Gordonsville the country.

Staying with my aunt that summer challenged me physically and emotionally. For the first time in my life, I had to use a communal outhouse for bathroom facilities. You could smell its foul odor before you even opened the door. There was no running water or electricity in Aunt Dot's house. So, we used oil lamps for light, and the men of the family retrieved water from the well for our daily use.

As if that wasn't challenging enough, I was now under the same roof with the family I felt rejected me. My parents had good intentions for sending me there. They simply wanted me to get to know my siblings and extended family. However, I was still processing my feelings and struggling with abandonment, something my young mind did not know how to understand. So to me, I was being forced into a very uncomfortable situation with people I did not know nor did I want to know.

To protect myself from the disappointment of not being accepted and liked, I reverted to not speaking unless it was absolutely necessary. I often cried, especially when Maggie would leave me to hang out with her friends in the area. It was a very trying time for me, and I believe Aunt Dot knew it because she sent me back to Covington early.

When I returned home, the residue of the emotional stress began to show. I often had visions of someone trying to get me and was afraid to go to certain places in our home. I would get my friends or cousins to go with me into those areas, especially the second floor of our house.

Then, my mother had Esther come to Covington a couple of times. Her goal was to help us get to know each other. But I was so angry and hurt I didn't want to talk to or share my things with her. I always felt that Esther and my other bio-siblings knew something about me that they weren't telling me.

My parents attempted to send me to Gordonsville for my summer breaks. Unfortunately, it always ended the same. Finally, after a week or two, my aunt would call my mother and tell her she was sending me home. Maggie would stay, but I would return home with my parents.

Back home, my mother put me to work in her beauty shop. She would have me wash her client's hair, which I didn't like doing. So, on occasion, I would not place my hand at the client's neckline, allowing water to run down their backs. I hoped my mother would think I was terrible at shampooing and give me something else to do, but that never happened.

After a few days, my hands began to break out. It turned out I was allergic to some of the ingredients in my mother's hair products. So, to my excitement, I was relieved of my duties as a shampoo girl.

My mother kept a watchful eye on me and did her best to find other activities for me during the summer.

Finally, she decided to send me to a predominately white camp in Millboro, Virginia. This time it was for work, not fun.

The attendees at this camp were white children, and the workers were mainly black. I worked as a waitress in the dining hall serving the parents of the white attendees. My duties were to clean and set the tables before serving the food. Being shy and timid, I was afraid during my first few days on the job. But as time went by, I became more comfortable waiting tables. The $20 tips helped motivate me too.

In addition to waiting tables, I was responsible for washing dishes and mopping the floor. I didn't like that as much. So, I paid the young guy working with me to do those chores for me. While he was doing the chores, I played my record player and practiced dancing.

My sleeping quarters were in a cottage at the top of ten dark, creepy stairs. To make matters worse, I could hear animal and owl sounds throughout the night. Then, as I walked to work on the other side of the camp, the cows and horses would chase me across the path. I was so afraid that I called my mother several times to ask if I could come home.

She would say, "Trisha, I'm sorry. You have to stay until the summer is over."

The summer nights felt long, and since I wasn't getting anywhere with my mother, I eventually called Aunt Tina for support. I asked her to come to pick me up, and she did. My mother was furious with her sister, but I was relieved.

In the end, I gained some great takeaways from my time at the camp. I learned how to wait tables and, despite leaving early, I faced my fear of the animals. But the biggest lesson was how to communicate and interact with strangers, especially those of a different race.

Chapter Two

Around June 1965, before starting my eleventh-grade year of high school, my mother hired a young man named Joe to tend to our yard weekly. He'd mow the lawn and take care of the flowers and plants in our yard. Joe was tall and slim, and my mother would always tell me how much of a nice guy he was. I, on the other hand, did not care for him or like him. Some days I would get the water hose and spray him in hopes that he would go away and never return. Of course, that didn't work because he was getting paid to take care of our yard.

No matter how many times I said no, Joe kept asking me to go out on a date with him. After my mother's encouragement, I finally said yes. On our first date, Joe took me to a party and brought me home drunk. I had such a bad hangover. I had to stay out of school for two days. My mother was furious.

She asked Joe, "What did you do to my daughter?"

Joe responded, "She only had one drink of vodka."

My mother said, "But she doesn't even drink liquor. Please do not give her any more liquor. As a matter of fact, she will not be able to go out with you anymore. You disrespected my daughter."

That was the end of me going out with Joe, so it seemed.

Later, I found out that Joe and some of the guys in Covington had made a bet to see who would get to take me out first. Well, Joe won the bet, and despite my mother's wishes, he wasn't going to give up that easily. Not long after the fallout from our first date, Joe came and asked me to be his girlfriend.

I said, "In order for you to date me, you need to buy me an engagement ring, a pair of diamond earrings, and a diamond necklace."

Joe responded, "Ok."

A week later, we went downtown to the jewelry store on Main Street to pick out all the jewelry I requested.

Once that ring was on my finger, Joe became very possessive and jealous. He was older than me and had already graduated. I was a junior in high school and was enjoying life as a teenager.

In addition to doing yard work, Joe worked at the local paper mill. It was the stinkiest place in Covington and made the whole area smell like rotten eggs. He worked the evening and night shifts. While Joe was at work, I would attend parties in the city with my friends. Then, he would get mad, leave his job, and come to where I was to take, or rather make, me go home.

We'd argue all the way to my house. Once there, he

would put me out of the car, making sure I went in the house before he left to return to work. Once I knew he was back at work, I would go back to the party. Then one of his friends would call and tell him I had come back. Joe would hang up and call the establishment and argue with me about leaving and returning home. It felt like a never-ending battle.

Joe was very controlling and acted as if he was my father. I was both fearful of him and angry with him to the point that I began to dislike him. I didn't realize it at the time, but I was in a toxic relationship. On many occasions, I would give back his engagement ring out of anger and frustration.

My parents noticed the unhealthiness of our situation and would often say, "You all fuss and argue too much. You need to take a break from each other."

As I look back, I realize that I went with Joe for the wrong reasons. I loved the things he could give me, but I was not in love with him. It was an unhealthy relationship from the start. My parents tried to warn me of the dangers ahead, but I ignored them, blinded by my false perception of love.

IN AUGUST 1966, Watson High School was forced by law to integrate with Covington High School. Going from segregation to integration was a radical change, and it upset and devastated many of the black students, myself included. While the integration of the schools provided a better quality of education and a change in some social and ethnic prejudices, we were excluded from participating in all extracurricular activities. For me, this meant no more basketball, no more cheerleading, just academics. This was especially hurtful because it was my senior year of high school.

Upon graduation in June 1967, I was accepted and enrolled in school to become an Airline Stewardess in Missouri. I was so excited about the opportunity to travel and see other parts of the country. My mother paid the tuition, but then she changed her mind.

She said, "It's too cold and too far away to go there for school."

Angry with my mother, I began to set another plan in action.

Maggie graduated several years before me and moved to Washington, DC, with our aunt Hannah. Maggie got married and moved into her own place. I knew that if I really wanted independence from my mother, I would have to get out of Covington. So, I called Maggie.

I said, "Maggie, Mother has decided not to let me go to flight attendant school. I just don't want to stay here. I feel like I'm stuck in prison. Please come and get me and take me to DC with you."

To my surprise, she agreed and a few days later came to get me. Although my mother was not pleased with my decision to leave, she didn't object since I would be under the watchful eye of Maggie. Joe was not happy about me leaving either. He tried to talk me out of it, but my mind was made up.

I was eighteen and headed to my new home in the nation's capital, and I had no plans to return to Covington. Maggie and Abraham lived on Kennedy Street, NW, in a one-bedroom apartment on the 3rd floor of a red brick building. The living room was my bedroom, and a green roll-away couch served as my bed. Since I didn't have a job, I did a lot of the cooking and cleaning to help out around the apartment.

Our neighbor, Shirley, across the hall, was very helpful in getting me acquainted with the area and learning the bus routes. Shirley introduced me to a guy named Jonathan, who became my best friend. Jonathan would take me around the city to parties and protect me from the bad guys in the area. When Jonathan wasn't available, my brother-in-law would drop me off at various parties and pick me up afterward.

Joe would come to DC at least twice a month. He would always accuse me of going out and dating one of his friends. This resulted in many quarrels. On one occasion, I had to call the policeman because Joe got very aggressive. This was another sign that Joe was not the right man for me.

WHEN I STARTED my job search, I was led by a family friend to take the Civil Service Test. I took the test, passed on my first attempt, and obtained a job at the Labor Department as a Clerk Typist, GS-2. This was the beginning of my tenure in the Federal Government. I started going to night school at Strayer University, taking shorthand. Within one year, I was promoted to a GS-3.

I felt it was time to spread my wings, so I began searching for a new job. I was hired at the Federal Trade Commission as a Clerk Stenographer. This job gave me room to promote up to the GS-5 level.

I was a part of the typing pool, which consisted of about twenty women. Our primary duties were to type up documents and take shorthand for the attorneys. We also transcribed tapes from the attorneys.

As I got to know some of my co-workers, I met and became good friends with two of the ladies. When one of us was called in to do shorthand for an attorney, the three of us would go in together.

The attorneys asked, "Why are there three of you here?"

We responded, "Well, we are one another's backup. So, if one does not get all of your dictation, the other will."

They accepted our answer, and we continued with our process.

For lunch, we would go to the restaurant across the street to eat and play cards. Sometimes we'd go to the roof of the building and enjoy a few alcoholic beverages. We were so close we would even get together some weekends to play cards. Sometimes we played for money. I would distract them by telling jokes and making them laugh so I could win.

After I won, I would say, "Well, it's time for me to go."

They would get mad and say, "You always take our money and leave."

Our friendship helped me to grow and settle into life in the DC area. Soon, I was ready to move on from my sister's house and get my own place. The only problem was I still needed a little help to make the rent if I were to get an apartment.

By this time, Joe and I had been engaged for three years. So, I gave him an ultimatum.

I said, "We've been together for three years. It's time for you to make good on your proposal. So, either you marry me or go on your way."

Joe decided to marry me. My parents disapproved of us getting married. They felt we argued and fought too much. Nevertheless, my dad signed the parental consent form for me to marry Joe. They even offered to plan and pay for the wedding.

I remained in DC the weeks leading up to the wedding. For forty days, I didn't have an appetite or eat. I did not know the voice of the Lord at that time. In hindsight, I realized God was speaking through my parents, telling me not to marry Joe. However, I was young and did not know the difference between infatuation and true love. So, I married him despite the warnings, which was disobedience.

Chapter Three

On January 17, 1970, we were married at my grandparent's house in the living room. My two best friends, Elizabeth and Ruth, cried the whole wedding because they knew Joe had been unfaithful during our engagement. They were supportive of me, but they really didn't want me to marry Joe.

Our wedding reception was held in the building next to my mother's hair salon. Although it was a celebration, I still didn't have an appetite. At the end of the night, we headed to the hotel. Joe was drunk and reeked of the smell of alcohol. Once in the room, he passed out in a deep sleep, and my appetite returned. I called my mother to bring me some food, and she did.

Looking back, I believe this was a sign from the Lord. Since we had not consummated our marriage, I could have gotten my marriage annulled. Instead, Joe resigned from his job at the paper mill, and we traveled back to

Washington, DC, to start our life together as husband and wife.

We stayed with Maggie and Abraham until we found our own place. Meanwhile, Joe began his job search. We found a two-bedroom apartment on Longfellow Street in NW, DC. The rent was $150 a month, and we were able to get approved on my salary.

To ensure we could sustain living on our own, I helped Joe get a job at the Federal Trade Commission, where I worked. In the beginning, working together was good, but after several months, Joe became jealous of my rapport and relationship with my colleagues. As a result, he started trouble with some of our co-workers and made false accusations. At that point, I began to look for another job and acquired a position with the Department of Transportation as a Secretary in the Chief Counsel's Office.

During the early days of our marriage, we would go home to Covington to visit our parents and friends at least twice a month and for most of the holidays. We would party with our friends, drinking, dancing, and eating good food while having fun talking and laughing about the past and the latest happenings. Joe and I shared the same birth month, which was May. So, we would hold parties at our apartment throughout May to celebrate. Our apartment was so small, and we could not let everyone in at the same time, so there would be a line of people outside in the hallway waiting to get in the party. They'd rotate in and out of the apartment, eating, dancing, and having fun. The drinks were free-flowing, and the music was loud. In addition to our house parties, we celebrated our birthdays at various clubs throughout the city.

We partied a lot, even outside of our birthday month. All the while, I was in college working on my degree. I would take my books to the parties and study between dances. I was determined to stay focused regardless of what was going on.

As I approached the final months of my Associate's Degree, I began to get sick at work. Then, one day, I came down with a severe case of nausea. I went to the doctor, and the sonogram showed I was six months pregnant with a baby girl. I was so upset. I felt it was the wrong time to have a child. However, despite what was going on in my body, I persevered and graduated with my Associate's Degree in Business Administration.

After seven months of pregnancy, I began to spot. It was determined that it was due to the stress of continuously being on my feet running errands at work. The doctor put me on bed rest and instructed me to start my maternity leave early. So, I went back home to Covington, where my mother could care for me.

Joe did not come to visit while I was in Covington. I was extremely depressed and upset. While I know he couldn't be there with me every day, he could have at least come to see and care for me on the weekends. I felt abandoned by him.

On December 7, 1973, I gave birth to a baby girl. The day before I had her, I walked around my neighborhood with Joe's uncle a few times. That night I began to have pains in my back. Concerned, I called the doctor.

She said, "You are in labor and need to get to the hospital immediately."

I always thought the labor pains would be in my stomach, but I soon learned that labor is different for each mother.

It seemed like my parents took forever to get dressed and ready to take me to the hospital, but we made it in time. However, Joe was still in DC and nowhere to be found. I was mad and upset that he wasn't there with me during the birth of our baby.

My girlfriend, Elizabeth, went to the hospital with us as extra support. I dilated so fast there was no time to get an epidural. So, they numbed me, and I had a natural birth. It didn't hurt as others had told me it would. However, I was relieved when it was all over.

I gave birth to a healthy baby girl at seven pounds and fourteen ounces. I named her LaShawn. It was a name given to me by Joann from my job, who I later appointed as LaShawn's Godmother. I stayed awake all night talking to the nurses and got to know them well over my three-day stay.

My parents came to pick-up me and LaShawn when we were released from the hospital. I decided to remain in Covington for a while longer, and that time was a gift from God. My mother cared for us as I recovered and taught me how to attend to my newborn baby. I was sore for a few days and had received stitches from the delivery.

But once my stitches healed, I was ready to get out of the house and have a little fun.

My mother watched the baby so I'd have a little time to hang out with my friends before heading back to DC After my six-week check-up, I returned to work and life in the city. However, LaShawn stayed with my mother for a few months while I looked for a babysitter.

Having LaShawn without my mother's help was a big adjustment. The pick-ups and drop-offs, diaper changes, feeding, and bath times all fell on me. Joe was hardly any help. He continued with life as usual, and his jealous temper continued to rage. He got upset whenever he had to take the baby to the doctor or the babysitter.

Our marriage began to crumble. Joe was very jealous of the baby.

He once complained, "We don't have any time for each other anymore,"

I asked, "What do you mean by that?"

He yelled, "We are drifting apart!"

I heard him, but there was so much to be done with a baby now. I tried to give him attention, but with his resistance to help with the responsibilities of the baby, I just didn't have the time or energy. To add to the stress, I was still taking classes at night to complete my Bachelor's Degree. At least he would watch LaShawn while I was at school.

I was blessed to graduate with my Bachelor's Degree in Business Administration from Strayer University in December 1975. It was only by the grace of God that I made it through. Taking care of the baby and the constant arguing and fighting with Joe was sometimes overwhelming. I almost wanted to quit school, but God.

~

ALTHOUGH JOE and I had gotten promoted to jobs in different agencies, we still rode to work with each other every day. We only had one car at that time, and we would argue over when and who was going to use the car. The front of the car was considered mine, and the back was Joe's. After dropping LaShawn off at the babysitter, Joe would drive to his job, and then I would continue to my job and park in the basement parking garage.

One day, I had picked up the checks for my office and was headed down Pennsylvania Avenue to pick up Joe for lunch. Suddenly, the car behind me started to blow its horn. I didn't understand what was going on until the car came up beside me.

The driver rolled down his window and yelled, "Miss! Your car is on fire."

Instantly, I panicked and slammed on the brakes. Then, I jumped out of the car and ran down the street. Then I remembered that I had left the checks in the car. So, I ran back to the car to grab the checks. By that time, the police officers and fire engines were on the scene.

The policeman asked, "Miss, did you set the car on fire?"

Confused, I responded, "No, sir."

I was terrified and didn't know what to do. However, I knew I needed to get back to work. So, I found a pay phone and called to let my supervisor know what had happened. After I got off the phone, the firefighters put the fire out, and the police took down my report.

We filed a claim with our insurance company, and they gave us a check for the car's value. Joe and I split the money in half, which was enough for each of us to buy a car. I bought a green Mercury Cougar with my money, but Joe decided to spend his money on something else. I was making the payments, and it was in my name. So it was my car, but here we were again arguing over a car.

Chapter Four

I n 1976, an upward mobility program opened up at my job. I applied to the program and was granted an opportunity to attend Southeastern University to pursue a Master's Degree in Public and Business Administration. This was a God-sent opportunity.

I was allowed to attend class during my lunch hour and work on my assignments while at work. I also attended classes on the weekend. However, the weekend classes were a little difficult with my duties as a mother and wife.

It was nothing but the grace of God that kept me and allowed me to maneuver through this time. I had all my day-to-day duties on top of trying to study and complete my schoolwork. I don't know how I would have made it through if it were not for God's hand on my life. Joe's help was minimal, and if he had his way, he would not have helped at all.

I remember this one cold winter morning when I was scheduled to take my comprehensive exams to graduate with my Master's Degree. After getting dressed for class, I headed down to the parking garage of our apartment building. Joe, with LaShawn in his arms, followed.

He stood in front of the car and said, "Where are you going this early in the morning?"

I replied, "You know I have to go take my exam."

He yelled, "You need to stay home with us!"

Our arguing echoed throughout the garage. It was so embarrassing. I'm surprised the neighbors didn't come down to see what was happening. Eventually, he moved and went back to the apartment.

Now, I was late and speeding, trying to get to school. Before I knew it, lights were flashing behind me, and the police siren was blaring. Frustrated, I pulled over. Not only was I extremely late, but now I had a speeding ticket to pay.

By the time I got to school, I was mad and flustered. When I received my test, my mind went completely blank. I couldn't remember any of the answers. The continuous arguing and fussing with Joe that morning had prevented me from thinking straight. Needless to say, I did not pass the exam.

I was furious. I immediately went to the Dean and shared what happened that morning. Then I asked for permission to retake the exam. Thankfully, my request was granted. This time, I passed the exam and received my final credentials for graduation. With much persistence and perseverance, I received my Master's Degree in Public and Business Administration in December 1980.

At the time of graduation, I was a Secretary GS-7, Step 10. Once I received my degree, I informed the personnel office that I had completed the Master's program and asked for a promotion. My desire was to work in the personnel office, but there were no vacancies. So, the Personnel Officer sent me to the Budget Office for a job.

When I met with the Budget Officer, he said, "There is no use in interviewing you because I was told you already have the job. With that said, you will be promoted to a GS-9 Budget Analyst with the potential to advance to a GS-13 in four years."

I was so grateful for the opportunity.

With all the great things happening for me at work, my home life became a battlefield. Joe became jealous of my accomplishments. He even went as far as accusing me of having an affair with my supervisor.

He said, "You must be sleeping with him. That's the only reason you got promoted."

From there, our marriage went downhill.

Joe came to my job on many occasions, starting arguments with me about minor things that could have been discussed at home. Several times, the police were called to the office to escort him out of the building. Eventually, he was banned from the building by the police. I was so embarrassed and, at times, feared losing my job because of his antics.

What's that old saying, "What doesn't come out in

the wash comes out in the rinse?" Well, I later found out that Joe was accusing me of having an affair because he was having one. It came through the grapevine that he was seeing a woman whose child went to the same babysitter as LaShawn.

Joe would start stupid arguments to leave home and would be gone for hours at a time. He wouldn't tell me where he was going or even call to let me know his whereabouts and that he was ok.

The confirmation came the day that LaShawn and I were riding with my friend, Lucy, and her daughter to the grocery store. They lived in our apartment building on the fourth floor. As we turned the corner onto Longfellow Street, I spotted our car, which by this time was an orange and black Monte Carlo, and Joe was opening the passenger side for a lady to get in the car.

As we drove by the car, I rolled down the window and yelled, "You better not come home tonight!"

Joe was unfazed and didn't acknowledge me. However, he must have heard me because he didn't come home that night.

The next morning, as he walked through the door, I immediately started my interrogation.

I said, "Who was that woman I saw you with yesterday?"

He said, "It wasn't a woman. That was one of my guy friends."

I said, "You opened the passenger door for a guy? Now, that's strange."

Joe replied, "Yes, it was one of my buddies."

Irritated by his lie, I remarked, "It looked like a lady to me."

He snapped and said, "Believe what you want too! I know who was in the car."

He brushed past me to go into the bedroom, and I did not say anything else.

Joe continued to leave and be gone for hours at a time. As if seeing him with that woman wasn't enough evidence of his unfaithfulness, I decided to follow him one night when he left. Sure enough, he was meeting up with another woman. This time I could not deny that he had a mistress.

Our marriage was now full of distrust and confusion. The arguing and fighting intensified so much that I had to call the police several times. My brother-in-law, Abraham, even had to intervene on my behalf at one point. Oftentimes, Joe would threaten to leave and move out.

Finally, I decided to call his bluff and said, "Ok. Well, get your clothes together, and I will take you to your friend's house to stay."

To my surprise, he got his clothes together and left to stay with his friend in Chillum, Maryland. This led to our legal separation.

Although Joe was out of our apartment, he would call every single day to curse me out and harass us. He called me all types of names. Then he'd call and say he wanted to come by to see LaShawn. Naturally, I granted his wish. Then, upon arrival, he would start an argument, and I'd have to call the police to escort him out of the apartment.

On one occasion, when the police came, Joe tried to take my car.

He said to the police, "I need to get my car out of the garage."

Since they were called to my house regularly, the officer asked to see the registration. After seeing that the car was in my name, the officer denied his request and immediately escorted him out of the apartment building.

We were in a toxic cycle, but I didn't know how to break it. However, I reached my breaking point the day Joe came by the house to get some of the clothes he conveniently left behind. The moment he entered the apartment, I smelled the liquor wafting from his breath. It didn't take long before he turned violent. He pulled out a gun, forced me into the bedroom, tied my hands, and raped me.

Terrified, I cried, "Why are you doing this to me?"

Never had I felt so helpless and stripped of my power. Joe held me in that room for at least four hours before he let me free and left the apartment. I was so devastated and heartbroken that I did not tell anyone what happened. Thankfully, LaShawn was away with a friend and not home during this drama.

Carrying this burden alone took a toll on me. After that ordeal, I didn't know what Joe was capable of next. I lived in fear and was very depressed. I began having chronic and severe headaches. My doctor informed me the headaches were a result of stress, anxiety, and fatigue, and he urged me to do whatever I could to get my stress under control.

After sixteen years of being with my high school sweetheart, we had come to this. Our good life had crashed because of his unfaithfulness as a husband and his controlling and possessive ways. Through the good and the bad, I stuck with him. Now I was left to raise our six-year-old daughter alone and unsure of our future.

I spent a lot of time crying and feeling lonely. Many days, LaShawn tried to console and cheer me up, but at her young age, she had no way of understanding what I was going through. To make matters worse, I started feeling sick and nauseous as if I were pregnant. Following my instincts, I went to the doctor, who confirmed that I was indeed pregnant.

When I broke the news to Joe, he was not happy.

He said, "Why would you have a baby when we are getting a divorce? I don't want you to have it."

I struggled, trying to figure out what to do. I was in a crisis and felt overwhelmed with emotions making this life-changing decision. Joe became impatient with me and began pressuring me to have an abortion. It was an unplanned pregnancy, and I was alone, scared, and confused. Unfortunately, I gave in to Joe's demand and had the abortion.

After my procedure, the doctor told me the baby was a boy. I was devastated! I had always wanted a baby boy to complete my family, and now he was gone. Honestly, I would have felt the same if it had been a girl. I didn't want to have an abortion, but I felt I had no other option. This sunk me into a deeper level of depression, where I had a hard time seeing my way out.

At work, my zeal had faded. I often spent my days sitting at my desk, trying to find my way through the fog of fear, frustration, guilt, and shame that plagued my mind. I wondered what was going to happen next. There were days when I would just sit numb and disconnected from everything happening around me. I daydreamed about what my life could be until thoughts of my reality crept in and blew my clouds of hope away. Then, knowing nothing else to do, I cried out to the Lord for Divine help.

I would soon learn how faithful the Lord is, for he heard my cry. One day, my friend, Anna, told me about a Bible study group held weekly during lunch in our office building and invited me to go with her. I accepted and, from that day on, attended faithfully. As a result, I, along with six of my friends who worked with me, surrendered our lives to the Lord Jesus Christ during one of our weekly prayer sessions.

I was so excited about my salvation. When I traveled back home to Covington for a visit, I shared the news with my family and friends during our get-together. I even took time to pray with people. I was partying with the purpose of spreading the good news of Jesus and my salvation.

As babies in Christ, consistency was important for our spiritual growth. So, my work friends and I met up to have Bible study and prayer service together outside of work. One of the more seasoned ladies from the job's Bible study group would come and teach us the Word of God. She taught us how to discern the voice of the

Lord and the spiritual gifts and talents he placed within us.

It was such a blessing to fellowship with them. We bonded at work and at home and even played on a recreational basketball team called the Transportation Express together. Our sisterhood was a blessing and just what I needed during that time.

In addition to dealing with Joe and his unstable behavior, I still struggled with grief, guilt, and shame from having the abortion. God knew my pain, and one night during a church service, he sent a prophetic word to me through an evangelist.

During the service, the evangelist called out, "There is someone here who had an abortion and is feeling guilt, shame, and unforgiveness toward themselves. But I want you to know that God is faithful and just. And he will forgive you if you repent and ask for forgiveness."

At that moment, I repented and asked God to forgive me for having the abortion. I felt in my heart that the Lord forgave me, and now I had to forgive myself. However, while the feeling of God's forgiveness was instant, it took me many years to find forgiveness for myself.

All the turmoil I had been through–the verbal, emotional, mental, and physical abuse led me to become a very bitter and angry woman. Although there were people around me physically and emotionally, I felt isolated and alone. I was weary and not sure how to see my way through.

Thank God for my friends and the Bible study

group. They prayed and stood in agreement with me that God would lift my burdens, strengthen me, and help me get through this challenging time in my life. With the strength of the Lord, I filed for divorce in October 1982 to finally end this toxic cycle.

Chapter Five

In December 1982, I received the call to the ministry. I was working on some budgets in my office when I experienced a divine interruption.

I heard a small inner voice say, "Get out a pen and paper and write this down."

I followed the voice's instructions, picked up my pen, grabbed a piece of paper from my yellow legal pad, and wrote down what I heard.

The voice said, "Go preach and teach my word."

While I was still learning the voice of God, I knew this was from the Lord. Immediately the scripture Isaiah 61:1-3 came to me.

It reads, "The Spirit of the Lord God is upon me, because the Lord hath anointed me to preach good tidings unto the meek, he hath sent me to bind up the brokenhearted, to proclaim liberty to the captives, and the opening of the prison to them that are bound; to Proclaim the acceptable year of the Lord, and the day of vengeance of our God; to comfort all that mourn; To appoint unto them that mourn in Zion, to give them beauty for ashes, the oil of joy for mourning, the garment of praise for the spirit of heaviness; that they might be called trees of righteousness, the planting of the Lord, that he might be glorified."

I accepted my call, and over the next few months, God intensified my prayer time and studying of his word. I continued to attend Bible study and prayer service weekly as well. I wanted to show myself approved by God.

One of my first assignments was to help those in need, which, in turn, would prove to help me as well. So, I started renting out one of the bedrooms in our two-bedroom apartment to those who needed temporary housing. LaShawn and I would share a room, and the other room, along with the living room floor, would go to renters for $35 a week.

On one occasion, I was led by the Lord to reach out to help one of my friends, Matthew, who lived in Washington State. He was having domestic problems and needed a change. So, in obedience to the Lord, I sent him a ticket for him to come to DC and stay with me and LaShawn.

Once here, Matthew gave his life to the Lord and was blessed with not one but two jobs. One job was at an investment firm, and the other at a transport company. He was doing so well. Then his wife came into town and started to harass him. They got into a bad argument, and he was arrested.

I was able to put money together to get Matthew out of jail, but he could no longer stay with me. While he was sorrowful for what happened, my family was still fragile and trying to recover from my broken marriage. So, he went to stay with a friend at Fort Meade. I later found out that he got a truck driving job and moved back to Washington State.

Although there were bumps along the way, I exemplified the love of Christ by helping those in need, just as my mother had done throughout my childhood. My mother always helped those in need with food, shelter, and clothing, especially the children. But this was only the beginning for me because God had more for me to do.

THE STATE of my marriage took a toll on me. Joe was out doing God knows what with whoever he wanted to, while I was stuck feeling unloved and rejected. So, I found love from another man who was also in an unhappy marriage. We bonded while sharing our marital issues, which led to us going to lunch with each other often. Lunch turned into dinner, then the movies, then vacations together, until we were having a full-blown affair.

Unfortunately, Joe's multiple affairs didn't make it right for me to break our marriage covenant too. After a while, I began to feel convicted by the Word of the Lord and ended the affair. Then, I went to God in prayer, repenting and seeking forgiveness.

I realized that I needed to be free of Joe. We both had been unfaithful in our marriage, and there was no reconciliation in sight. So, I agreed to an uncontested divorce that was granted and finalized in May of 1983, and the judge gave me full custody of LaShawn.

While it was a relief to see the toxicity coming to an end, it was also devastating. And if I'm honest, I do not want to go through that type of pain ever again in life. If you ever encounter that type of pain, I strongly encourage you to seek God for a heart of forgiveness. I discovered that holding all that anger inside only hurts you, not the other person, and unforgiveness is a heavy burden to carry.

I am ever so grateful that I went to counseling, especially after the divorce was granted. I had to let go of all the anger, unforgiveness, and bitterness in my heart. I had to release it all so that the Lord would forgive me. While it wasn't immediate and took some time, I eventually found peace in my heart, body, and soul.

Despite going through a divorce, the Lord was still tugging at me concerning the call to ministry. So, as God would have it, I joined Mount Gilead Baptist Church in downtown Washington, DC. Not long after, I was baptized again and received the right hand of fellowship. Then the Lord began to speak to me about going into full-time ministry. It was not something that I took lightly, so I stayed before the Lord, seeking confirmation. A month later, I resigned from my job as a Budget Analyst to prepare to enter full-time ministry.

Launching into full-time ministry did not go as

smoothly as I had hoped. Being divorced and unemployed, I could not keep up with my rent and other household bills. However, I'm grateful for my mother and how God used her to help me during this time of transition.

In addition to the $150 a month in child support I received from Joe, my mother gave me $150 monthly to help pay my rent. I applied and was approved for food stamps, which felt very humiliating at the time for someone who was used to working and earning their way. I realize now that it was my pride getting in the way because I felt like I was being judged for needing assistance.

We went a lot of days without money and gas to get around. Eventually, I had to sell my car for cash to get items that food stamps did not cover. During this period of my life, my daughter and I fasted a lot to be more sensitive to the voice of the Lord and because food was scarce in our house. Leaning on God kept us and gave me the courage to press toward the mark He was calling me.

In the fall of 1983, I delivered my initial sermon at Mount Gilead. My sermon was entitled "Take No Thought for Tomorrow," and my reference text was Matthew 6:25-34. Unfortunately, my pastor was ill and unable to attend the service. However, one of the Deacons stepped in and helped me through the nerves and anxiousness in preparation for the service. Many of my friends, co-workers, and family members attended the service. Afterward, I was presented with a license to preach the gospel of Jesus Christ.

Once I was licensed and had served as a minister in training for some time, my pastor encouraged me to go to seminary school. So, I applied to Howard University's School of Divinity and was accepted as a full-time student. The only problem was I didn't have any money for tuition, nor did I know where to get the money.

To my surprise, the church where I served paid for my first semester of school. Then, I received a scholarship that covered my tuition for a year. After that, I applied for financial assistance and was approved for a student loan, which helped cover the rest of my years in school.

Seminary school was such a blessed time in my life. I learned what it meant to truly trust and rely on God. It was also a time that allowed me to grow even closer to my mother. She was very instrumental and supportive of me during this transition in my life. I remember one semester, she went with me to register for classes. The lines were long, but she waited patiently with me.

Naturally, there were moments when my faith was put to the test. I did not have a babysitter. So, I had to take my daughter to school with me. Some days she would sit in the class with me; on others, she would sit in the library until my class was over.

Although I was on financial aid, there was a portion of my bill I was responsible for covering. I recall one semester when I had an outstanding bill. I knew it had to be paid and was doing my best to get the money together. Then one night, I had a dream a couple of nights before that the computers were shut down, and an angel went in and paid my bill before I registered for the next semester.

A couple of days later, I went to the school to pay the bill.

The registrar said, "Your bill is paid in full."

I asked, "How can that be?"

She said, "All I know is your account is paid in full. Please move on. There are a lot of students in the line waiting to be seen."

I did not question it anymore. I just thanked the Lord for making a way out of no way and moved on as instructed.

Depression began to wear me down, and it had layers to it. I was destitute in every area of my life—physically, emotionally, mentally, spiritually, and financially. I was still dealing with residue from my divorce, working with a reduced income after leaving my job, raising my daughter alone, and trying to be obedient to God's calling on my life.

One of the deacons from the church referred me to a Christian counselor. There I received counseling to help process the trauma from my marriage, divorce, and grief. During this time, I started to release fear, disappointment, anger, hurt, and bitterness.

God also blessed me with a good friend, Anthony. He and I met while attending Howard. He was a great inspiration and friend to me. He was in Divinity School to become a Chaplain. We would hang out as friends, and occasionally he would attend church with me on Sundays.

Then one day, Anthony became sick.

He called me and said, "Trisha, do you think you can bring me some food?"

At the time, I was cooking a little something for me and LaShawn.

So, I said, "Well, I'm cooking now. I can bring you a plate once I finish."

Anthony said, "No, I think I want some Popeyes. Yes, some chicken with a biscuit and a side of red beans and rice."

I laughed, "I'm cooking chicken now. But ok, I will get you some Popeyes and bring it over."

I cut my stove off and covered everything up. Then LaShawn and I headed out to fulfill Anthony's request.

A week later, he passed away from pneumonia. My daughter and I were so thankful that we obeyed the Holy Spirit at that time. Only the Lord knew what was going to happen. It was and is so important to know the leading of the Holy Spirit and to take heed, trusting and obeying the Lord.

Looking back, leaning on my faith in God saved me from a life of depression and grief. I courageously attended Christian counseling for two years. In exchange, I received courage, forgiveness, love, compassion, joy, peace, and strength.

If it had not been for the Lord on my side, walking with me and protecting me, I don't know where I would be today. And I am especially grateful for the angels that God put in my life to pray for and encourage me at that time. With their help and God's love, my daughter and I persevered through these trying times.

Chapter Six

After receiving counseling and releasing the past, I finally felt ready to open my heart and try being married again. So, I began to pray for a husband.

One of the deacons from my church always said, "Be careful what you pray for. You might just get it."

Well, I met Moses at church, and after courting for a short while, he proposed to me. However, I refused his proposal. He got upset, left the church, joined a cult, and followed them to North Carolina. He had diabetes, and listening to the leader of the cult, he stopped taking his medicine.

News got back to me about what was going on with him. After praying for him, the Lord led me to go to North Carolina to pick him up. However, just as I had refused his proposal, he refused to return to DC with me. The next thing I heard was Moses slipped into a diabetic coma and died.

I continued praying, asking God for a husband, and then while visiting another church, I met Jimmy. He told me that the Lord said that I was his wife. He, too, proposed to me.

I prayed, "Lord, is this the one you sent me?"

The Holy Spirit led me to have Jimmy take me and LaShawn to Baltimore Harbor. Naturally, I asked, and he obliged. While there, I saw a pregnant woman with two sets of twins. Upon seeing her, she immediately spoke a word from the Lord.

She said, "God said he is not your husband."

When I shared with Jimmy that God said he was not my husband, he was very sorrowful. Not long after, he got sick and died of a broken heart. It hurt my heart that Jimmy was hurt in such a way. I truly loved him as a brother in the Lord, but I thank the Lord for protecting me from marrying the wrong man again.

After dealing with Jimmy's passing, I decided it was time to step away for a little while. So, I took LaShawn, along with my friend Jackie and her son, on a trip back home to Covington for a few days. We loaded up the car and headed out.

We stopped by a nearby gas station to gas up and pick up a few snacks for the road. A guy named David came out to ask if we needed him to pump the gas. We agreed.

Then, I asked, "Can you also check under the hood and make sure we are good on oil too?"

After checking everything out, he said, "Ok, ladies, everything looks good." Then as we were about to leave, he said, "If you ever want your car detailed, I can do that too. Here's my number. Give me a call when you return home, and I'll take care of it."

I took his number, and we became good friends. I even got to know his uncle Calvin who also worked at the gas station. They were like guardian angels for me and LaShawn on many occasions. You see, even though Joe and I were divorced, he had a vendetta against me. He still tried to find ways to intimidate and harass me.

Joe was a very cruel and evil man. The jealousy and rage he displayed during our younger years only intensified throughout our marriage. Even though he was unfaithful throughout our time together, he did not want to see me happy or with anyone else.

After our divorce, Joe began to stalk and follow me around. Several times he tried to attack and kill me, but God used his angels, David and Calvin, to block him. I am so grateful for the support system that God placed around me during this time–counseling, friends, and family.

On one occasion, David and Calvin drove to Covington, along with me and LaShawn, to meet my mother. The trip was very pleasant, and my mother was happy to meet my two angels. Upon arriving back at my apartment in DC, Joe was in the garage trying to start a fight with me, but God and his angels were there for Divine protection.

Unlike before, I was wiser, stronger, and rooted in God and his word. I no longer felt fearful, helpless, and hopeless when it came to Joe and his schemes. God was my helper, shield, and protection; therefore, who could stand against me? So, I continued handling God's business while he handled mine.

The time came for me to start my field training for Divinity School, which was a prerequisite for graduation. To meet this requirement, I served as an Outreach Minister at a church in Northeast Washington, DC. The Outreach Ministry included the Street, Hospital, and Prison Ministries, and it had five active members, which were me and four other ministers from the assigned church.

On Saturdays, we'd do outreach ministry throughout the Northeast communities. Since I didn't have a car, many days, LaShawn and I would ride the bus or catch a taxi to church. There were even days when I was by myself that I would hitchhike to the church.

My Saturday would start with fasting. Then once at the church, the ministers and I prayed at the altar for God's Divine covering, protection, and anointing before going out in the field to do ministry. When we finished praying, we gathered our leaflets and headed out into the community to do spiritual battle.

One of our regular spots for outreach was the park on Eastern Avenue. We preached and taught the Word of God and afterward held an altar call to invite sinners to receive salvation. Many souls were saved, inspired, and encouraged. There were also many who received deliverance from alcohol and drugs.

DURING MY FOUR years of Divinity school, I obtained several temporary part-time jobs. While I know the Lord told me to leave my government job to pursue full-time ministry, it was a serious challenge trying to live solely off public assistance. I had to find some additional way to supplement my lack of income.

There was a time that I worked at a group home taking care of three mentally challenged men. There, I prepared meals, assisted the supervisor of the house with various tasks, and took the men to church on Sundays for their spiritual growth.

When that job expired, I went to work as a receptionist at Howard University radio station for six months. Knowing that this job was temporary, I took the post office exam. Although I passed, there were no vacancies at that time. So, I continued to apply for various government jobs.

In 1986, I got a six-month position at the Federal Home Loan Bank Board (FHLBB), where an employee was going out on maternity leave. The night before the interview, I had a dream. In the dream, I saw a blue IBM typewriter sitting on a desk.

When I went in for my interview the next day, I saw the same blue IBM typewriter from my dream sitting on the desk where the selected candidate would sit. At that moment, I knew that was my job. Sure enough, I received a call saying I had been selected for the position.

While working at FHLBB, I built a great rapport with my supervisor. I worked hard and ensured that I completed my assignments in a timely manner. After the six-month period was up, I went to the personnel officer and asked if there were any permanent job openings. The personnel officer made a telephone call, and I got a GS-7 Secretary job without even applying. I knew that this was nothing but the favor of the Lord.

Although there were many traumatic and trying times during my school years, the Lord blessed me to graduate in June of 1988 with a Master's of Divinity from Howard University School of Divinity. Within a year after that, I became an ordained Baptist Minister.

The blessings continued to flow from my time at FHLBB. While working there, I met a young lady who told me about a housing program in Montgomery County. A year later, with her help, I applied and received a $500 voucher to rent a house in Silver Springs, MD. In addition to the rental voucher, we received a voucher for electricity and gas.

LaShawn always wanted to live in a house. Now, the Lord was answering her prayer. After living in an apartment for 18 years, I left Washington, DC, and moved my daughter into her dream home in Silver Spring, MD. We pulled up to Carona Court, and there it was LaShawn's dream house.

It was a four-bedroom brick front townhome with a fully finished basement that included a bedroom, closet, full bath, a washer and dryer, and a recreation room. There were three bedrooms upstairs with two full bathrooms and large closets in each room. My bedroom was on the front side of the house, and LaShawn's room, along with our guest bedroom, was on the other side, facing the backyard. The first floor had a living room, dining room, half bathroom, coat closet, and a kitchen with a bay window. To top it off, we had a small backyard and a nice mid-sized front yard with two assigned parking spaces right out front.

Once we were moved in and settled, I started holding prayer services on Saturdays for the women and men of God from different churches. We came together for two hours to pray for each other's needs and world issues. Following that, we would have scripture readings led by the Holy Spirit and light refreshments to restore nourishment to our bodies. Many of the saints were healed, delivered, and set free during our prayer sessions.

In addition to the weekly prayer services, I returned to renting to those in need. This time I could rent out my basement, which was like a little apartment of its own. One of my renters was a friend of a fellow church member, Butch. At the time, he was in the police academy and had been going through depression and financial problems. As the Holy Spirit led, I often prayed for and ministered to him.

Once Butch graduated from the police academy, he changed and became very controlling over me and my daughter.

He would say things like, "You all are staying out too late. You shouldn't be going to church across town. You should be home."

Then, he started answering my phone.

He would tell callers, "It's too late for you to be calling Trisha."

Finally, I said to him, "It's time for you to leave. You need to start looking for another place to stay."

To my surprise, he began to cry. While I understood his disappointment, there was no way I could tolerate that type of controlling behavior. God had delivered me from that type of relationship, and there was no way I was going back to it. So, he got himself together and saved enough money to get his own place.

Once Butch moved out, I was able to maintain the house rent and bills for a bit without the extra income. However, by the time the holiday season came, we had reached a point where we had no food to eat. One evening, I set the table by faith, believing the Lord would give us a miracle. To my surprise, the telephone rang, and it was my father-in-the-Lord calling from Lancaster, PA.

He asked, "Do you all need anything?"

My daughter, in the background, yelled, "We need some food!"

He said, "Well, what do you need?"

I quickly gave him a list of the foods we needed. Without delay, he traveled to our home in Maryland and brought all we had given him on our list. That night, I cooked us a nice dinner, and he stayed to eat with us. I graciously offered him our guest room for the night so he wouldn't have to drive back to Pennsylvania. It was a glorious fellowship that showed us the love and favor of the Lord, for surely He is an on-time God.

Thanksgiving and Christmas came, and the Lord continued to bless us. Our holiday season was filled with lots of joy and food. Family and friends gathered at our townhome to celebrate the holidays, and the Lord provided.

Chapter Seven

After working at FHLBB for a while, the Lord led me to look for another job. This time I found a Budget Analyst position at a different federal agency. I was interviewed by one of their female supervisors.

After reviewing my resume and asking me a few questions, she said, "I am going to give you a chance."

The Lord once again showed me favor. I was hired as a Budget Analyst at the GS-12 level. With this job, I was restored to the salary I had when I resigned from my job back in 1983. I was so grateful that my faithfulness and perseverance had come to fruition. Now with confidence, I proclaimed that God is a God of Restoration.

Over the course of a year, God restored my finances, and life was turned around for me and LaShawn. I continued to pour into the men and women of God, and God continued to restore me—mentally, physically, and emotionally. Finally, things were coming together, and I was grateful to God for his hand of favor on my life.

Then, after a year of working as a Budget Analyst, my supervisor began to harass me about doing church work and getting a job as a counselor.

She would say, "You are in the wrong field. You need to be working in a church somewhere or find a job as a counselor."

This became such a constant thing that it made me uncomfortable. The straw broke after she gave me an unsatisfactory performance appraisal rating and tried to demote me. There was no way that I was going to accept that. So, I filed an EEOC discrimination complaint on the grounds of race, color, religion, sex, and harassment.

Unfortunately, the results were not in my favor. After reviewing the case, EEO determined that it was not a case of discrimination but more of a need for communication and reconciliation. So, my supervisor and I were required to meet once a week to try to reconcile our differences.

The sessions were very unproductive. We would sit in her office and look at each other.

She would say, "Is there anything you want to say?"

I would reply, "No. Is there anything you want to say to me?"

She would respond, "No."

Then we'd sit there for the rest of the hour saying nothing to one another. This went on for weeks, and we were getting nowhere near a resolution.

Finally, I began seeking God through prayer and fasting for an answer on what to do. At God's leading, I began to look for other employment opportunities, but this time in the counseling field. To my dismay, I wasn't selected for any of the counseling jobs for which I applied. So, I went back to God in prayer.

Then, I came across an opening for a Chaplain Intern at St. Elizabeth's Hospital in Southeast Washington, DC. I applied for the position and was called in for an interview. There were three Supervisory Chaplains that sat in on my interview. If chosen for this position, I would work with individuals with acute mental illnesses who needed intensive inpatient care to support their recovery.

Well, the Lord's will was done, and they offered me the position, which I gladly accepted. While it was a paid internship, the stipend was only $18,000 a year. So, I took a $15,000 decrease in salary. However, I wasn't worried because I knew God would provide just as he had done in years past.

Five days a week, I commuted an hour and thirty minutes to work from Silver Spring to Washington, DC, for my intern position. With the decrease in salary, often, I would run out of money in between pay periods. I didn't know where to get the money for gas and food.

The uncertainty during this time of transition often occupied my thoughts so much that I could not pay attention during the intern group sessions at work. The students, as well as the instructors, noticed that I was preoccupied. One day, they pulled me up in a circle.

They asked, "What's going on with you, Trisha? You are often distant and unengaged with the group."

As humiliated as I was, I broke down and told them about my financial problems. Immediately, the students began to show love and compassion toward me. I was given monetary donations from the group.

After that group session, each morning when I arrived at the hospital and checked my box, there was an envelope with money in it to buy gas and anything else I needed. I learned a great lesson from that experience. Sometimes, we must swallow our pride and ask for what we need.

On Sundays, I had Chapel Duty. LaShawn would often tag along with me while I ministered to the patients and brought them down from their rooms to the chapel for service. Once service was over, we'd take the patients back to their respective areas. Most of my patients suffered from acute mental illness. However, a handful of patients were considered criminally insane and housed in a locked-down ward. Of course, only the acute patients attended chapel service.

It was a great experience for me and my daughter. We both learned a lot about those who suffered from mental illness and their needs. We decided rather than calling them mentally ill; we would call them special people with special kinds of needs.

Upon completing the Chaplain Intern program, I obtained five units of clinical pastoral education and began looking for a full-time Chaplain position. The only problem was I could not find one. So, I began to look for other positions on the campus of St. Elizabeth's. I found out that there was an Alcohol and Drug Center on the grounds. Remembering my days in the park ministering to those with alcohol and drug problems, I walked over to the center to see what positions they had available.

I entered the building and walked over to the receptionist.

I said, "Hello. Is the Director available?"

The receptionist was kind enough to get me some time with the Director.

I asked the Director, "Are there any vacancies?"

She replied, "There is an opening for an Alcohol and Drug Counselor."

I said, "I do not have any experience as a counselor, but I need a job. I'm willing to go to training to receive the hours to become a certified Alcohol and Drug Counselor if you give me a chance."

She paused, then said, "I will give you a try."

The Director brought me on as an Intake Specialist. Once I completed the counseling certification courses, I was moved to the position of Alcohol & Drug Counselor. I oversaw a GED class and relapse prevention. I also counseled clients one-on-one, wrote treatment plans, and held aftercare classes. In addition, it was my responsibility to take the men and women in our center to the Narcotics Anonymous (NA) and Alcohol Anonymous (AA) meetings held on the campus twice a week.

Our center worked on shift schedules, and I alternated between day and night shifts. There were three sides to our recovering addicts' housing– female-only, male-only, and co-op. The men were very respectful and cooperative, but the women gave me a lot of grief.

Once I acquired a license to drive the center's van, I

took the men and women out to different functions within the city. I formed a men's choir, and they traveled with me when I preached at various churches throughout the city. I tried to do the same with the women, but that did not work out. One night, I took the women to a service with me, and they became very disrespectful and uncooperative. So that was the last time I took them out of the dorm.

Chapter Eight

1991 brought some great experiences for me and my family. I journeyed into the career field of Counseling, and my daughter graduated from high school. It was an exciting time with new experiences on the horizon.

After graduation, LaShawn expressed that she did not want to go to college. However, Joe and I felt different. Despite my rocky past with Joe, LaShawn was now old enough to make her own decisions about having her dad in her life. While Joe and I didn't see eye to eye on many things, one thing we did agree on was that we wanted our daughter to continue her education. She'd have better opportunities with a college education when she entered the workforce.

LaShawn obliged us and applied to Bowie State University. She was accepted, and when fall came, she moved to campus and started school. Things seemed to be going great initially, but we discovered she was failing around mid-semester. She had been skipping classes to hang out with her boyfriend. It was obvious that forcing her to stay in college would only be a waste of time and money. So, after she completed that semester, we didn't make her go back.

Not long after, LaShawn became pregnant. However, she did not tell me. Instead, God showed me she was pregnant in a dream. It was later confirmed when her friend's grandmother informed me that LaShawn was planning to abort the baby. Immediately, I prayed and asked God to intervene and stop the abortion.

I was very upset and angry with LaShawn. I didn't understand why she didn't come to me for help and to discuss what was going on with her. This was also a trigger for me. It took me back to the same regretful decision I made some years ago. So, I gathered up LaShawn, her girlfriend, and LaShawn's boyfriend, Ronnie. I took them to our home in Silver Spring, and that night, I prayed with them, and they repented and accepted Jesus in their lives.

A few months later, on September 13, 1992, LaShawn went into labor. I was with her at the hospital when she gave birth to a beautiful baby girl. At the time, LaShawn had not picked out a name for the baby. As I held my granddaughter, I sang a song to her entitled "Gotta Find Me An Angel."

The nurse overheard me singing and said, "Why not name her Angel?"

LaShawn thought about it, then agreed, and that is how Angel got her name.

After Angel was born, LaShawn decided to move to an apartment with Ronnie, and I became an empty nester. From time to time, I would babysit Angel for LaShawn. Although I had work and ministry duties to fill my time, I missed the constant companionship. This alone time made me desire to be married again. I had completed counseling and been delivered from the trauma. I truly felt like I was ready for this next step.

Then one morning, as I moved about the house, there was a knock at my door. I opened it to find a strange man standing on my front stoop. He introduced himself as George.

Then he said, "I know this may sound strange, but the Lord told me that you are my wife."

I replied, "Well, the Lord didn't tell me that."

We talked a bit more, and from there started to spend a lot of time getting to know each other. We even attended church services and prayer meetings together.

After some time had gone by, I decided it was time to make things official. So, I asked for an engagement ring, and George agreed. Then, we went to the jewelry store to pick out my engagement ring. He purchased it right on the spot.

Things were progressing with my relationship with George, but on my home front, life was changing in a big way. I received a notice from my landlord that my rent was going from $500 to $1,000 a month. After taking the huge pay cut in salary, my budget could not afford the increase. Saddened, I began to pack my things. I sold most of my furniture, including my washer and dryer, to generate extra money until I found a place to go.

My uncle, Bill, from Covington, called one day, and I shared with him my housing situation.

He said, "Well, Trisha, you know your sister Esther lives in Lanham, and from what I heard, she's having financial troubles and is about to lose her house. Why don't you see if you can move in with her? Then you'd have a place to stay, and you could pay rent and help her save her home."

Now, Esther was my younger biological sister. We weren't close, but my uncle was right. This was an opportunity for us both to help each other out in our time of need. So, I called Esther, and she agreed to let me stay with her.

My time with Esther turned out to be such a blessing. Living together helped us develop a sisterly bond and get to know each other better. In the end, I had a stable place to stay, and Esther could keep her house and catch up on her monthly payments.

Things hit a snag with George when I found out he would sometimes park outside of Esther's house, watching to see what I was doing and where I was going. Then, he started complaining about me working at the Alcohol and Drug Center. He especially didn't like it when I had to work night shifts in the men's ward.

Things escalated all the more after I was stuck at work for 36 hours due to a snowstorm. It snowed so bad that no one could leave or come onto the campus. So, we had to stay overnight until the roads and parking lot could be cleared enough for the relief staff to make it in.

George's jealous behavior was very familiar to me. We wanted to get married but agreed we should go through premarital counseling first. My cousin was a pastor in Baltimore, Maryland, so we scheduled a counseling session with him.

After our first session, George said, "He is too close to family. We have to find another pastor to counsel us."

So, George's pastor referred us to another counselor.

After three sessions, the pastor said, "For homework, I want you both to write down ten things you do not like about each other."

We went home, and we both independently made our list. When we returned for our next session, we presented them to each other. This exercise would be the tip of the iceberg that we were on course to hit. Our interest in getting married started to fade after that session, but we continued to maintain our relationship.

Not long after, I was led by the Lord to tell George that he had a calling on his life as a Minister. He answered his calling and took steps to prepare for ministry. A few months later, he preached his initial sermon at his church in Clinton, Maryland.

George seemed to be turning over a new leaf as he moved into his ministerial calling. But then I discovered that he was still drinking and smoking cigarettes. Things started to come to a head when he received a DWI, and his driver's license was revoked. I had to drive him around like a chauffeur until his fines were paid and his driving classes were complete.

Once George's driving privileges were restored, he then began to come and pick me up to take me where I needed to go. At first, I thought it was simply repayment or gratitude for all I had done for him while he didn't have a license. However, it turned out it was simply a tactic of control. George was very jealous and possessive of me. He got to the point where he would not allow me to drive anywhere by myself.

I remember one day, we were in the car driving over the Route 50 bridge. As we were arguing, his car broke down in the middle of the bridge.

I asked George, "Do you have anyone that can come and pick us up?"

He replied, "No."

We walked to a nearby payphone, and I called my girlfriend, Jackie, who lived around the corner from my house, to come and give us a ride. She came and took George to his house in Clinton and then took me to my house.

Before I got out of the car, Jackie turned to me and said, "Trisha, this is not someone you want to marry. You don't want anyone who cannot take care of you."

The Lord was speaking through Jackie, and I was listening.

Not long after, I caught George in a compromising position. One Wednesday night, I went over to his house to pick him up and found him with another woman in his car. With no real explanation as to who she was, this led to mistrust and, eventually, our breakup. I later heard from one of his friends that he married an usher from his church.

About a year later, George died due to one of his lungs collapsing. I was not invited to his funeral or told when it would be. His death saddened me. But God's grace was sufficient for me during my time of grieving, and I was able to move on.

The bad news seemed to keep coming. After four years of working at the Alcohol and Drug Center, my job was abolished in April 1995. I returned to part-time, temporary work as a Receptionist at Howard University's radio station with the hopes of becoming a regular full-time employee. However, before my three-month assignment at the radio station was up, I got a call from the U.S. Postal Service. They offered me a part-time job as a Letter Carrier, working 32 hours a week.

I was assigned to a post office in Montgomery County, and I carried mail for 89 days in the rain and many hot days. The Postmaster would ride around and watch me deliver the mail. One day she came over to me while I was working my route.

She said, "You seem to be having a hard time. Do you want to deliver mail for the rest of your life?"

I said, "No."

She said, "Ok. Well, I will terminate you, and you can apply for an indoor job."

I was so upset when she terminated me, but as a parting gift, she gave me instructions on how to apply for an indoor job with The Postal Service. I followed her instructions and was granted a Markup Clerk position in an office with twelve other automation clerks in Capitol Heights, Maryland. While working as a markup clerk, the employees would strike and stop working. The supervisor noticed that I had the skills to make the clerks work. I was nominated to become a Supervisory Team leader on several occasions and worked mandatory hours on several occasions.

While working at the Postal Service, I moved out of Esther's house and in with LaShawn and Ronnie. Although their apartment was about 45 minutes from my job, I felt this would be a good time to bond with my LaShawn and Angel.

I slept on the floor in Angel's room for about six months. Then, LaShawn and Ronnie decided to get married. After dating for several years, they were married on July 1, 1995, in their apartment. Many of our family members and friends attended the wedding. They had a lovely reception at a reception hall in Prince George's County, paid for by Joe.

Once LaShawn was married, I began to look for a place to stay closer to my job. One of the clerks, Charlene, overheard me talking to another co-worker about wanting to find a place to live closer to the job. Then she offered me a room living with her and her daughter for $150 a month. It was an offer I felt I could not refuse. So, I accepted, packed up my things, and moved to Waldorf, Maryland.

Like all young couples, LaShawn and her husband had a few tough times. Joe and I would help them as much as we could, especially Joe. When LaShawn's husband needed a job, Joe helped him find one. When they needed a car, Joe helped them get one. Joe always came through when LaShawn needed him, and I was glad to see him present and involved in LaShawn's life. LaShawn was very grateful to her father for his love and compassion toward them during their difficult days of marriage.

Chapter Nine

On January 23, 1996, my beloved mother passed away. Even though I knew she was up in age, it was still a shock to me. With dad gone and Maggie and I living in DC, there was no one back home to take care of her. So, Mother moved to DC to stay with Maggie.

After Mother developed dementia, Maggie was no longer able to take care of her. We had already moved her sister to a Nursing Facility in Maryland, so we moved Mother into the same facility. They both lived out the rest of their days there.

I was sure to visit them both when I went to see Mother. I'd sing my mother's favorite hymns to inspire and encourage her. She always smiled to show appreciation and lightly tapped her hands in rhythm.

I will always remember my mother's everlasting love for her children, her nourishing support, and the legacy of faith that she passed down to me. She instilled in us the age old saying that only the strong will survive. My mother gave the best hugs and ended every conversation with I Love You. I will forever hold her memory in my heart, for she chose to love me when no one else seemed to. Mother's life was celebrated at Covington Baptist Church, and then she was laid to rest at Cedar Hill Cemetery.

After my mother's estate was settled, we received a financial inheritance from her. The inheritance was split between me, Maggie, and Joshua. I saved up a little nest egg while staying with Charlene. So, my savings plus the money I received from my mother's estate was enough for a down payment on my first home. So in the spring of 1998, I began my search for the house that would be the perfect fit for me.

My realtor and I went all around the DC Metropolitan area looking at condos, townhomes, and single family homes that fell within my approved budget. I did my best to stay encouraged and prayerful while going from house to house. Finally, I put a contract on a townhouse in Severn, Maryland.

I was so grateful for my time at Charlene's house. Her kindness in allowing me to stay with her and her daughter allowed me to pay off my debt and save money. Charlene was a great blessing to me during the year and a half I stayed with her.

In May 1998, I moved into a new beautiful brick-front 3-level townhome. It had three bedrooms, two and a half bathrooms, and a grassy front yard enclosed by a white fence. A living room, dining area, and kitchen were on the first level. There were a few steps up to the second level, where there were two bedrooms with carpet, one full bathroom, and a laundry room. On the third level was a large bedroom with hardwood flooring, a walk-in closet, and a full bathroom.

As if purchasing my first home wasn't exciting enough, a couple of months after I moved in, LaShawn and Ronnie purchased a townhome around the corner from me. It was such a blessing having LaShawn and her family so close to me. On the weekends, we would get together to have family meals. Then on the holidays, we would alternate houses to host family and friends to celebrate.

They lived in their townhome for about three years and then expanded to a single-family home in Upper Marlboro, Maryland. I was devastated when they moved away. It felt like I was an empty nester all over again. So, I started renting out my second level to friends and family in need.

As in times passed, my home became a place for the prayer warriors to gather and go before the Lord on various matters. On Saturday mornings, intercessors from different area churches would join me in laying before the Lord for the people. We would intercede for marriages and singles, for souls to be saved and delivered from addictions, world problems, politicians, and other issues that God brought to our spirit.

I recall one instance where we had an all-night prayer lock-in. There were five of us, and we slept on the carpeted floor of the first level. We prayed all night until we got a breakthrough knowing that the Lord heard our prayers and would answer speedily. We woke up early the next morning, cooked bacon and eggs, toasted bread, with coffee and orange juice. We blessed the food and broke bread together. Afterward, we discussed the Word of God and shared what the Holy Spirit revealed to us during the prayer. Then, it was time to depart. The benediction was said, and they left to go home.

THINGS WERE GOING WELL with my job at the Post Office. Over the years, I got to know my coworkers and made some great friends. Naturally, I prayed with them and shared the good news of the Lord whenever possible, and they were fully aware of my past experiences as a Chaplain and minister.

The great thing about working at the Post Office was that the employees came from diverse backgrounds and walks of life. In my area, there were four veterans that worked with us. One day, while at work, one of the veterans came to me and shared a Chaplain vacancy they had come across.

He said, "Hey Trisha, I came across a vacancy for a Chaplain and thought about you. You want the information so you can apply?"

Excited, I replied, "Yes!"

He passed along the vacancy information, and I applied for the position.

During my interview, I shared with the Supervising Chaplain and his assistant how I saw in a dream that I would be working there. Ultimately, in September 1999, I was hired as a part-time Staff Chaplain for the Baltimore center. However, to supplement my income, I continued to work at the Post Office until I moved into a full-time Staff Chaplain position the following September.

After ten years of waiting, I was finally working my dream job. God answered my prayer in his perfect timing. Every job I had and all the ministering I did over the years was training and preparation to become the Chaplain God wanted me to be.

The Lord gave me favor with the supervising Chaplain. He later told me that he mainly hired me because of the dream I shared with him about me working there. My confidence in telling them I would see them later stuck with him, so he hired me. That God confidence resulted in me making history as the First Black Female Chaplain in Baltimore and Perry Point, Maryland.

I worked between the Baltimore and Perry Point VA Medical Centers as a Staff Chaplain and Substance Abuse Counselor. Thankfully, my new home was only sixteen miles from the Baltimore facility. I was considered an essential employee, so I had to report to work even on snow days during the winter months. I'm so thankful for my neighbors who helped dig me out on those days so I could report to work.

Things were going well at the VA. It was an honor to serve and help those who put their lives on the line to serve and protect our country. Over time, I got to know many of the men and women as they came in for their appointments.

One day while at the Baltimore center, a gentleman, Samuel, who I had met and seen around the center a few times, came up to me to talk.

He said, "The Lord told me that you are the woman I've been looking for."

I laughed and said, "Oh really."

We continued to talk a bit more. Soon after, we started to spend time together outside of the center. Samuel introduced me to his mother, his sister, his brothers, and some of his other family members. We often celebrated Thanksgiving and Christmas with his family at his mother's house.

I remembered the day Samuel proposed to me. He got down on his knees and asked me to marry him.

I laughed and said, "Are you serious?"

He stood up and said, "Yes, I am serious."

Then he got back down on his knees and asked again, "Now, Trisha, will you marry me?"

Without hesitation, I said, "Yes!"

We went to the jewelry store to pick out a wedding set for me and a band for him. We hadn't picked a date, but we were prepared for when we did.

Samuel was very supportive and attended various services with me when I was out ministering at different churches proclaiming the gospel of Jesus Christ. Samuel and I prayed and studied the Bible together regularly. However, I noticed a pattern when we attended prayer services together.

There came a time when every time Samuel would attend prayer service with me, he would have symptoms of a heart attack. The ambulance would be called, and they'd take him to the hospital. Come to find out, he was using drugs, and they were causing him to have these symptoms. These were warnings from the Lord for Samuel to stop using drugs, but he refused to heed the warnings.

In addition to his many medical conditions, Samuel also struggled with mental, family, and financial issues. His family often said that he went into the military and came back a different person. Not understanding everything he was going through mentally and emotionally put a wedge between Samuel and his family. As a result, he often felt rejected and abandoned by his family, which caused him to become depressed and turn to drugs for an escape.

Samuel had to be hospitalized several times and could not find a job. He wasn't unable to receive his service-connected benefits, so he applied for Social Security Disability and was denied several times. So, he hired a lawyer who helped him win his case, which included a lump sum of money for back pay. But Samuel was not a good steward over his money. In all of his spending, he did not tend to the important things he needed.

I began to pray for Samuel's salvation and deliverance. After hearing a sermon at my church in Silver Springs, Samuel accepted Christ, joined the church, and was baptized. However, things changed after Joseph joined the church. It's like he lost his appetite for God and no longer wanted to go to church.

Tensions rose between Samuel and his family. He became very combative and began to stay out late at night using drugs more heavily. Then he cried out to the Lord, and the Lord heard him and delivered him out of all his troubles (Psalms 34:18). Samuel's social worker intervened and advised him to go to a drug treatment program in West Virginia for nine months to help him get clean. I fully supported Samuel during his recovery process.

Upon completing the program, Samuel was supposed to attend NA meetings, obtain a sponsor, and go to aftercare to maintain his sobriety. However, he did not. Instead, he blew off his aftercare plan and therefore relapsed. His behavior caused a lot of wear and tear on our relationship.

After three years of engagement, Samuel and I separated and called off our engagement. Samuel didn't handle our breakup well. He became very depressed, and his health went downhill. He did not take care of himself and was hospitalized many times for drug abuse and heart problems. He just could not break the habit, and it amplified his Post Traumatic Stress Disorder (PTSD) and sped up the deterioration of his heart.

Chapter Ten

For most of my life, I felt unloved and rejected by some of my family members. I desired a strong and positive relationship with all of my adopted and biological siblings. I wanted to spend quality time with them. I wanted that close-knit relationship where we supported one another through difficult challenges and life's day-to-day events.

Life taught me the importance of creating and having a stable core family unit. Life has so many twists and turns, and having someone to lean on and trust in times of trouble and despair helps to fight depression and loneliness. The human connection is sometimes undervalued, but we must remember that God did not intend for us to walk through life alone.

For many years, I could not find that kind of relationship within my own family, and I now realize it wasn't all my family's fault. I ventured outside and began to isolate myself from them based on the hurt and pain caused by certain family members.

I prayed and sought the Lord on what to do.

The Lord answered, "You have a family in the body of Christ. I have many who will love, support, pray with you, and have compassion for you in your time of need. My Word will help you in times of brokenness, despair, and pain."

Each day, I embraced God's family more and more. I connected with my church family, friends, neighbors, and members of my community at large. I spent time with the families of my friends and acquaintances, admiring their close relationships with each other. I attended their family reunions and family holiday gatherings partaking in the enormous amount of love they expressed and shared with one another.

While I was grateful for the family of God, the older I got, the more I hungered and thirsted for a close family relationship with my biological siblings. The problem was I didn't trust them. I felt they were holding back information and keeping family secrets, especially regarding my birth father.

Although my mother tried to bridge the gap between me and my biological siblings after my birth mother's death, I was still hurt and didn't want to have anything to do with them. God healed my relationship with my sister, Esther, when I went to live with her. However, there was still work to be done with my other biological siblings.

Esther thought it would be good for us to visit our

oldest sister, Donna. I didn't know what to expect, but I was open to seeing how things would work out. So, we took a trip to New Jersey to spend a weekend with Donna.

When I look back on that trip to New Jersey, Isaiah 43:19 comes to mind. God was doing a new thing with me and my sisters, and I embraced every moment as it unfolded. During our stay, we bonded as we had never done before. We swapped childhood stories, and to my surprise, it wasn't as painful or awkward as I had imagined. Somehow hearing their stories helped my anger and hurt subside. I left Donna's house feeling loved and accepted. That weekend was the new beginning I had prayed for with my family.

Over the years, my relationship with my ex-husband Joe improved, so much so that I would even say we became friends. We partnered together in raising LaShawn as she got older, and I believe we gained a different level of respect for one another. Joe even started occasionally attending the church where I served as an Associate Minister. The Lord blessed one Sunday, and I was able to lead Joe to Christ while he attended church. He didn't join the church right away, but around 2008 he joined the church and was baptized.

Joe became very active in the church and even became a Trustee. I thanked and praised the Lord for answering my prayer to save Joe. Through this experience, I learned that nothing is too hard for God. In life, we all will go through trials, tribulations, and challenges that will build our character and teach us how to always trust and depend on the Lord.

In June 2014, Joe died from cancer. I thought the loss of my ex-husband would be very devastating. But to my surprise, it was not as difficult as I assumed. I believe it was because I was at peace knowing we had reconciled and that Joe knew the Lord before he passed away.

A couple of years before his passing, Joe was diagnosed with cancer. At first, he didn't disclose to me or LaShawn what was going on with him. Eventually, he started treatment and could no longer keep the news from us. Joe suffered for a year and a half, going back and forth to the doctors and the hospital.

Despite everything we had been through, I prayed that his sickness would not be unto death. I knew that it would be devastating for our daughter and grandchildren. If I tell the truth, in the beginning, we had some great times and some good ones in the end too.

Many of Joe's friends were steadfastly by his side during his illness. LaShawn and our grandchildren often cooked his meals and spent time bringing him joy despite his pain and suffering. The day Joe passed, his best friend of many years was by his side. She called LaShawn to let her know his time was very near, and in turn, LaShawn, crying, called me.

LaShawn asked me to go to Joe's home and minister to his friends and family. I agreed and arrived just in time to pray the end-of-life prayer. This was extremely difficult for me, but the Lord empowered me to do what was needed. I knew that Joe was going to heaven because I had seen his growth in the Lord.

Joe was a good-standing member of the church until he could no longer attend due to his illness. It was very devastating watching him suffer. On his deathbed, he asked for my forgiveness, and I accepted his apology. I now understand that his apology was a release for not just him but me as well.

We had a great homegoing service for Joe at a funeral home in Glen Burnie, Maryland. A busload of his friends came from Covington, Virginia, to join his family, friends, and church members for his services. In the end, Joe was a well-loved man.

In one of our last conversations, he said, "Trisha, you make sure you do the work the Lord has assigned to your hands."

His encouragement meant a lot, and even today, I know the Lord brought me through all of what I had been through to do just that–the work he has assigned to my hands. But for a moment, that light dimmed. See, during the time of Joe's death, God gave me the strength and peace needed to be there for my daughter and his family. It wasn't until later that I began to grieve.

Just as my heart was beginning to heal from the loss of Joe, another devastating loss headed my way. A few months later, as I sat in the hairdresser, I received a call from Samuel's sister.

She said, "Trisha, Sam's gone."

Samuel had a heart attack while at the hospital receiving treatment. I was in shock and couldn't believe my ears. My heart instantly sank. Although we had called off our engagement, I still loved him and had hoped that one day we could find our way back if he ever got clean. But that day would never come now.

With sadness, I hung up with his sister. Then, I turned and shared the heartbreaking news with my beautician and those in the salon. Many of them knew him because he would often come with me to the salon when we were together.

Despite Samuel's drug habit, we had some great times together. When he was sober, he was fun, loving, and supportive. Now he was free from the pain, sickness, and torment that kept him so bound.

God allowed me the honor to officiate Samuel's funeral to help celebrate his life. I had hoped it would help bring closure, but it did not. With the grief from Joe's death still lingering, Samuel's death added an unspeakable void to my heart. I felt empty and stuck.

My previous pastor suggested that I see a grief counselor to help me process my feelings and emotions. He also shared that connecting with others in a support group would be a powerful healer. So, I followed his advice and contacted a grief counselor to help me with the grieving process.

So many have touched my life and now gone on to be with the Lord—my biological Mother, adopted parents, brother, and many other friends and family. I have had so many deaths occur in my life that left me feeling sad, angry, empty, numb, guilty, and regretful. I'm grateful for the Godly wisdom I learned from my Godmother and my big sister in the Lord. They were there with words of comfort and strength from the Word of God during my difficult days of grief.

The individual and group counseling sessions were also a tremendous help. The first piece of advice my counselor gave me was to let time be the healer and to remember that this, too, shall pass. Then, my counselor listed several coping strategies to have at hand when the grief reared its ugly head.

The strategies she gave are as follows:

1. Write down thoughts about loved ones, whether a letter to send them or happy memories you could refer to when the pain arises.
2. Turn to family or friends.
3. Rely on your faith.
4. Maintain ample sleep and a healthy diet.
5. Take time out for enjoyment.
6. Gratitude heals at deep levels, so count your blessings and be grateful for what you still have.

My biggest takeaway was that when we love, we must learn not to live without our loved ones but to live with the love left behind. The only way to get over death is by seeing it as a life completed instead of a life interrupted.

As the Apostle Paul said in Philippians 3:13-14, "Brethren, I count not myself to have apprehended, but this one thing I do, forgetting those things which are behind and reaching forth unto those things which are before, I press toward the mark for the prize of the high calling of God in Christ Jesus."

Grief comes in many forms and impacts people in various ways. It is important to remember that allowing oneself to grieve is a healthy part of healing. There is a time, space, and place to process grief. Sometimes it's hard to express how we really feel. However, learning and identifying the best way to process your feelings will aid your healing process.

Throughout the transitions of grief in my life, my faith and trust in the Lord sustained and comforted me. It was not always easy, but I am grateful for the time I had with every one of my loved ones that I've lost. They may be gone from my sight, but they will never be gone from my heart.

DAVID and I had been friends for years. We had become such good friends that, at one point, he and his son, Junior, came to live with LaShawn and me. At the time, both LaShawn and Junior were in high school. Although David lived with us longer, Junior only stayed with us for a few months. Then he went to live with his grandfather. David and his father didn't have a good relationship, so he was unable to go with Junior when he moved.

A short time after, David decided to move in with his girlfriend. She was heavily into drugs and was horribly cruel and wicked. After David moved in with her, he got caught up in her lifestyle of drugs and alcohol, and it almost cost him his life. One night, David was so high he jumped out of a third-floor window. He survived that, only to be thrown out of the window of a mid-rise building a year later, fracturing both of his feet.

I knew something had to be done and that he could not continue living like this with that woman. So, I intervened and went to David's father for help. I begged him to mend their relationship and allow David to come live with him for about a year. They were able to sort out some of their differences, and David's father agreed to let David stay with him while he recovered from his injuries.

David stayed with him a few weeks before coming and asking to move back in with me. I didn't want him to go back to that woman, so I allowed him to move back in. Knowing that he was safe and not using drugs gave me peace of mind.

God did some great things with David while he lived with me. One Sunday, while David was still in a wheelchair, he attended church with me. He wanted to go to the altar for prayer, so I wheeled him down the aisle. After praying the prayer of faith, he received healing from his drug addiction.

Things were starting to look up for David. At the time, he was unemployed and receiving Social Security. In an attempt to get back on his feet, he applied for disability. His application was approved, and he was able to get his own apartment. He was able to maintain his independence for about a year but somehow became homeless again. Without giving much detail, he asked if he could come back to live with me, and I agreed.

David was such a good friend and helped me many times over the years. He was there during my separation and divorce from Joe. He was there when I preached my initial sermon. He was my sounding board and cheerleader when I transitioned and became a full-time Chaplain. When I had to travel for ministry, David helped me pack and iron clothes. Despite his shortcomings, David was a great friend to me and always there when I needed him.

Imagine my surprise when I found out David wanted to be more than just my friend. Sometime after Joe's passing, I was packing and preparing to travel for a ministry event. In the middle of talking and ironing clothes, David stopped and proposed to me. I did not turn him down. However, I gave him a list of things he needed to do before I seriously considered his proposal. He accepted the terms but never proposed to me again.

Even though David moved on to date other people, we remained great friends. Until this day, he checks on me often and comes to me when he needs an ear or spiritual guidance. If I don't know anything else, I know he is a true friend sent by the Lord, and I am so glad to have him in my life.

Chapter Eleven

I worked a combined total of 46 years in the government and private industry. I knew I could retire, but I loved working as a Chaplain. Then, to my dismay, I suffered an injury on the job. On two separate occasions, I fell at work and badly injured my knees. The second fall was worse than the first. I had to file for workman's compensation and attend physical therapy.

I cannot truly express the pain and agony that I experienced. I went back and forth to the doctors and physical therapy visits for so long. I even attended acupuncture sessions for pain relief. After a while, my x-rays showed I had osteoarthritis in both of my knees. Then an MRI confirmed that I had the start of arthritis in my lower back. At that point, I was referred to an orthopedic specialist in Baltimore, Maryland.

I began corticosteroid injections and hyaluronic acid injections as treatment for both knees. They worked for about a year, but then the agony returned. So, I went to three orthopedic specialists in Baltimore, MD. They all recommended a total knee replacement, but I wasn't satisfied with their answers.

I heard the Holy Spirit speak to my heart and say, "You do not need surgery."

So, I got a 4th and 5th opinion from two other orthopedic specialists in Waldorf, MD, who stated that I did not need a total knee replacement.

One specialist said, "Your pain level is not high enough for surgery."

The other specialist said, "You do not need surgery. However, you will need to get orthotics in your shoes to support your knees and back."

I was relieved by the report that I didn't need surgery. I truly believed God was going to heal my knees and back.

However, my relief was short-lived as I began to have issues with the veins in my legs. I embarked on a six-month journey filled with procedures to correct the blood flow in my legs. During this time, I felt alone and abandoned. I went through many of these procedures by myself.

Often, I remembered how I prayed for and sat with many others who were having surgery and procedures. Now, it was my turn, and no one was there to support or pray for me.

When I mentioned how I felt to my doctor and the nurse, they said, "We are here with you for support and are praying you have a successful surgery and a speedy recovery."

I began to battle feelings of complete exhaustion. If I tell the truth, I had been feeling this way for some time, but I continued to push myself. The tiredness was coupled with feelings of depression, irritability, loss of creativity, and the desire to often withdraw from others.

The reality was I had been through a lot over the past several years. The death of loved ones, health issues, and financial ups and downs caused me to feel battle fatigue. But I didn't quite know how to deal with it.

The exhaustion even affected me spiritually. My zeal for God faded, and at times so did my faith. I didn't want to preach, teach, pray, or sing anymore. I was in such a slump that I couldn't focus while in service and often left feeling discouraged. At the time, I took this as a sign that it was time for me to move on. So, I terminated my membership at my church.

I was restless and bored with life. I felt trapped in a cycle of unproductiveness, and I didn't understand why. I've always loved my job as a Chaplain, and I have always had a heart to serve God's people. But now nothing mattered anymore–not my health, not my job, not ministry, nothing.

As I distanced myself from others, they distanced themselves even more from me, or so it seemed. That angered me and allowed the enemy to creep in with the narrative that I had been used and taken advantage of by those around me.

Norman Shawchuck & Roger Heuser stated, "Caring for yourself while serving others is very important for self-care."

I finally realized that I had not been taking care of myself. I spent so much time serving others and managing the hills and valleys of my life that I had not truly checked on me. As a result, I was now in a state of complete burnout.

At the realization that I was burned out, the Lord led me to take a sabbatical and go to a place of solitude to pray, rest, and be refreshed by Him. I looked up the meaning of a spiritual retreat and found it was a set time with God away from the everyday noise and pressure of life for spiritual transformation. Retreats allowed you to get into a posture to hear clearly from God.

Immediately, I began to search for a place to retreat and obey God. I discovered a resort called Williamsburg Plantation that was a few hours outside of the Washington DC Metropolitan area. After visiting, I purchased a timeshare with them. It became a place of retreat for me to commune with God while surrounded by his beautiful scenes of nature.

Upon arrival at the resort, I disconnected from all technology. I wanted uninterrupted time in God's presence. Each day of my sabbatical, I arose with intense worship and prayer. I fed my spirit with God's word for spiritual growth and refreshed it with praise and worship. I repeated this daily. God restored, rejuvenated, and refreshed my soul with each passing moment. He constantly reminded me that no matter the circumstance, He was always with me.

When I returned home from my sabbatical, I had a clear mind, my stress was reduced, my health improved, and so did my mobility. I started encouraging my colleagues to take sabbaticals to recharge and regain perspective. That time away reignited my passion for ministry and helping others. It also opened my eyes to other opportunities that awaited me, such as traveling, writing a book, seeking additional education, etc.

Pushing through burnout only led me to brokenness. I now understand that we must regularly take time away to reconnect with God so that He can renew and direct us to the next level of our journey in Him. Without this time, we become numb and deaf to God's voice, leaving us at the mercy of a continuous unproductive cycle.

TOWARDS THE END OF 2015, the Lord spoke to me and said, "It's time to retire."

While it wasn't new news, it wasn't necessarily what I wanted to hear. When I was away on my sabbatical, the thought of retirement came to me. However, I had no idea what to do with myself once I retired, nor did I want to think about it. Being a Chaplain was my dream, and I had lived that dream for 17 ½ years.

Nevertheless, being obedient to what I heard the Lord say, I went to my supervisor to inform him I was ready to retire.

He responded, "Can you wait until April?"

I said, "Let me pray about it, and I will let you know."

I went to the Lord in prayer and asked the Lord if I could work until April and then retire.

The Lord said in my spirit, "My grace is sufficient for you."

So, I continued to work with the expectation of retiring in the spring.

Approaching the end of my career sparked a roller coaster of emotions within me. There was a part of me that was happy and excited about new possibilities, but then there was another part of me that was sad and filled with anxiety toward the unknown. How would a life of leisure feel after four decades of working? Would I have enough money to support myself, or would I go back to struggling and barely making ends meet? Questions of what if and how constantly plagued my mind the closer I got to my retirement date.

LaShawn was very supportive of the idea of me retiring.

She said, "Mama, retirement is the best choice you can make at this point in your life. You've worked your years, and now you have a chance at a new beginning. Your latter days will be far greater than your former. Just think, you'll be able to spend more time with me and your grands. I thank God for your release from work!"

I said, "I don't know. What if I don't have enough money in retirement to live on? Then, I'll be right back where I started."

Lashawn said, "Count up the cost of your monthly living expenses, then let go of your unbelief. Don't worry. It's time for you to retire and enjoy your life."

Angel joined in with her mother and said, "Grandma, this is just one chapter of your life closing. Seek God on what to do next. It may also be a good idea for you to see a counselor. They can also help guide you in the direction of your next."

Over the years, I helped many adapt to life changes, and now I was challenged to deal with my own major transition. Truth be told, I realized that although I loved it, I had grown to a place of tiredness in my spirit from being on the wall daily, pouring out prayers, words of encouragement, love, and counseling to those ready to give up on life.

Even though I was not ready to retire in my heart, I went to the personnel office to put my papers in for retirement in April. The personnel office went over my retirement pension and benefits with me. To my surprise, based on what they showed me, I would be able to cover my monthly expenses. My daughter was right. If I put my trust in God, everything would work out just fine.

My job wouldn't be the only thing I was preparing to say goodbye to. After seventeen years in my home in Severn, MD, I was led by the Holy Spirit to sell my townhome. My bedroom was on the third level, and it took me 35 steps to get to my room. I was getting older, and my knees could no longer handle the stress of all those stairs. I needed a home with one or two levels and fewer stairs.

In my heart, I really didn't want to move and let go of my lovely townhome and neighborhood. This had been my home, and the community was the nucleus of my life.

My church, friends, and favorite shops were here. This community had become family to me. Moving meant I would have to start all over again; at least, that's how it felt.

LaShawn referred me to her realtor, who was a God-fearing woman. In obedience to the Lord, I called and scheduled a consultation with her. The realtor came and walked through my house. Then we talked about my expectations and what I was looking for in a new home.

After our meeting, she said, "Ms. Bell, can I be honest with you?"

I replied, "Yes, please do."

She said, "I don't think you're ready to let go and put your home on the market. If I do it now and you're not ready, your house will not sell. So, when you let go of your home in your heart, give me a call. Then, I will put it on the market, and it will sell."

I took a few days and thought about what the realtor said. She was right, and I knew I had to make this move. So, I prayed and gave it to the Lord. Then, I called her up, and the search started.

The realtor took me to several places throughout the Maryland and DC areas, but we could not find what I wanted. Finally, after searching the Internet for new condos and townhomes, I found a new housing development for Senior Citizens in Waldorf, which was in Charles County, Maryland. The community had single-family homes and villas with one and two levels.

I told the realtor about the development I found, and we went down to tour the new community. They were building a phase of homes that would be completed by the end of the year. It was a 55+ community with elegant, spacious homes and exceptional amenities. It had a clubhouse that included an indoor/outdoor swimming pool, fitness room, men's and women's locker room, recreation room, and a sitting room for reading.

I fell in love with the Senior community and knew it was where I wanted to live. So, I put a contract and deposit on one of their Griffin model homes. Then, my realtor put my house on the market. The purchase of my new home was contingent on the sale of my current home. Therefore, it was essential to find a buyer willing to go to closing around the completion of my new home.

I was so excited about my soon-to-be new home. It was the first home I contributed my input on the design. Over the months it took for the house to be built, I watched as my home was built from the ground up. I visited the building site at least once or twice a month. My daughter and the realtor went with me to pick out the flooring, cabinets, and other fixtures for the home. I prayed over my home and the community I would soon be joining.

On December 30, 2015, I went to closing on the sale of my townhome. The nice couple also bought my bedroom furniture, dinette set, and a few other items that I left in the townhome. The next day, I went to closing and purchased my new charming two-story brick-front villa in the Waldorf Senior community.

My new home had three bedrooms, and two and a half bathrooms, with the master suite on the first level.

Upon entering the front foyer, I was greeted by beautiful wood floors, a vast mahogany wood stairway with beautifully designed balusters, and a long hallway that started at the base of the stairway. As you followed the hallway, you were led to living spaces located in the rear of the house.

The first floor of the villa included a half bathroom, a kitchen with granite countertops, a laundry room, and access to a two-car garage. In addition, there was a spacious dining and living room area with beautiful high-arched windows that allowed cozy daylight to brighten the room.

The owner's suite rounded off the first level of my new home. It included a full bathroom with dual sinks and a walk-in closet. On the second level was a carpeted loft, two bedrooms with walk-in closets, a full bathroom with dual sinks, and a large storage area. Then, outside was a spacious backyard with a white fence and a round patio with flowers on both sides.

My best friend and neighbor, Jackie, helped me to transition from my home in Severn, Maryland, to Waldorf. She stayed up with me all night packing and paring down for the move to my new villa. On move day, it was all hands on deck. Jackie, a few neighbors, and a couple of my friends from Baltimore helped me load up the truck and head to Waldorf. Once I moved in, Jackie and my friends from Baltimore came down for a few weekends to help me unpack and set up my new home.

I had to get used to my new community and environment. It was a small town but very busy. There was a lot of traffic getting in and out of the area. At that time, I was still working in Baltimore, MD. It took me about two hours to get to work in rush hour traffic, and traffic coming home was no better.

The commute alone took a toll on me. The rubber-necking often caused me to get tired and sleepy while driving. I knew I didn't have much longer before I retired, so I asked Jackie and her husband if I could stay with them until I retired. They agreed, and I stayed with them in Severn, Maryland, during the week and went home on the weekends.

It was so nice staying with them. They treated me as if I were a part of their family. Staying with them reminded me of how much fun and love I used to have when I stayed with LaShawn and her family. They were very hospitable and supportive and helped me prepare for retirement.

Chapter Twelve

On April 30, 2016, I retired from the Veterans Medical Center Chaplain service. My supervisor had a retirement party for me and another Chaplain retiring at the same time in Perry Point, Maryland. I cried as I gave my farewell speech to my colleagues.

During my farewell speech, I shared what a great learning experience it had been helping, healing, inspiring, and sharing coping skills with the Veterans and staff members. I closed my speech with the confession of how it would be a great task adjusting to retirement and finding new meaning and purpose in my life. Then, I prayed a blessing for all of those present.

Now that I had retired, it was time for me to return to my new house. Jackie helped me pack up the things I had accumulated at their house. Again, I was flooded with mixed emotions. See, had I retired in December as originally planned, I would have only been retiring from my job. Now, I was leaving my job and my best friends of over forty years, and it saddened me.

The roots of our lives were so entangled. Our children grew up together, and our husbands were best friends. My friends had been by my side through some of the most challenging times in my life. No matter what I was going through when I needed them, they were there for me. We laughed together, cried together, and kept each other encouraged through life's ups and downs.

Although I was only moving about an hour away, it felt like I was losing a part of myself. I grieved leaving their home. I wanted to cling to them because they were important to me, but I knew I had to let go. How conflicted this transition made me feel. They were still living, but I felt sorrow as if they weren't. I reminisced on all of the good times we shared, traveling, celebrating the holidays, attending worship services, and going to fellowship with other friends in the neighborhood.

Our social connection had been an essential part of my well-being and emotional health during the transition of retiring and moving to a whole new community. Friendship with others, in general, had proven to benefit my mental and physical health over the years. In addition, the shared discoveries and opportunities to lean on others greatly impacted my life.

I realized the apprehension I felt toward this transition in my life stemmed from fear–fear of the unknown and fear of losing the bond and connection I had with my friends, coworkers, and church family. This fear was so gripping, at times, it overrode my willingness to be obedient to this move of God in my life.

In an attempt to reason with the Lord, I asked, "How can I praise you in a strange land?"

That's when God took me back to his word. He reminded me that he is always with me and would never leave me or forsake me (Deuteronomy 31:8) and that He did not give me a spirit of fear (2 Timothy 1:7). It took a lot of prayer and standing on the promises of God to adapt, adjust, and embrace the changes in my life.

Marilyn Monroe once said, "Sometimes good things fall apart, so better things can fall together."

My life felt like it was falling apart, but it wasn't. I had to adjust the lens of this situation to get a new perspective on my life. To do that, I visualized the new friends and connections coming my way. It was scary, but I was open and receptive to embracing the new things God had in store for me.

As for my old friends, I wasn't losing them. I just had to make the most of every moment I was able to spend with them, be it by phone or the occasional visit. So that's what I began to do, make every moment with them count. It was the age old saying, quality over quantity.

MY FIRST FEW months of retirement prompted major changes in my identity. It created an enormous emptiness in my self-worth and sense of purpose. Retirement was hard. I had a whole lot of time to do nothing, and all I seemed to do was think about all the time I had to do nothing. My mind was idle, and it certainly became a playground for negative thoughts and feelings.

When I decided to retire, Philippians 4:11(b) is the scripture I stood on.

It reads, "For I have learned to be content whatever the circumstances."

I followed that up with Matthew 19:26.

It reads, "Jesus looked at them and said, 'With man this is impossible, but with God all things are possible.'"

So, with God, I took the leap of faith and retired. I left with joy and perseverance, thinking that retirement would be the best time of my life. But it wasn't turning out that way.

I had to learn that retirement was a journey, and as much as I wanted instant answers, I had to take some time to figure everything out. I was grief-stricken, unsure of who I was now, and emotionally all over the place. Talking to a close friend and journaling helped, but I stayed in prayer, seeking the face of the Lord, trying to find rest in him. As the days and weeks passed, I learned how to accept that I had retired.

Thankfully, I still attended counseling regularly. So, I scheduled a session with my counselor.

I said, "I don't like retirement. Everyone keeps telling me I will get used to it, but I don't know. I feel rejected and seen but not heard. I don't know what to do without the structure that employment gave me every day. At this point, I'm contemplating going back to work part-time to regain a sense of purpose."

The counselor said, "Patricia, you are in the first stage of retirement, which we call the 'honeymoon' stage. It normally lasts about a year or two. Describe the other feelings you are having?"

I replied, "I feel depressed, lonely, and anxious. I feel like I've lost my purpose." Then, crying, I continued, "Lord, help me!"

The counselor sat quietly for a moment, then said, "Patricia, I know it feels hard, but you have to let go of the past to move forward into this next chapter of your life. I have an assignment for you. I want you to take some time and list your goals for the next five years, along with the steps you need to take and the time frame needed to accomplish them."

Over the next few weeks, I found it hard to set goals for the next five years when I didn't know how to be structured for twenty-four hours. I was in constant prayer and repentance because I spent most of my time pleasing others and not doing what I truly desired. This left me feeling angry at myself. I had to regroup and start a new, balanced life. It was time for me to help myself and work on my goals and new purpose in life.

I realized that I was free from the bondage of working for someone, the hustle and bustle of traffic, rushing to get to work on time, and heavy workloads. I had transitioned to a life of independence with the ability to do whatever I pleased.

As I looked back over the years that I worked, I shook my head and yelled out, "I thank God for freedom and deliverance from work."

Although I struggled through many long hours on my previous attempts to write down my five-year goals, I returned to the table with a new perspective. I discovered that I needed to rest, relax, and be refreshed by the Lord. After hearing me toil over setting my goals, my counselor drilled down even more and advised me to work on my spiritual, physical, mental, social, financial, and relational goals. My retirement became a time of new priorities and interests. This was a great difference in how I looked at retirement.

Life became a stage that allowed me to focus on things important to me. I valued family, friends, and loved ones more than ever. I realized that retirement did not change who I was but gave me a sense of connection with people. It also gave me the ability to use my gifts and talents in a positive way. With this new point of view, I obtained fulfillment and control over my daily schedule without pressure.

Chapter Thirteen

After I purchased my home in Waldorf, I knew it would be necessary to transfer my church membership from my church in Severn, MD. As with the other parts of this transition, it was not easy to let go. This ministry played a major role in my life during my time as a Chaplain.

My pastor was very supportive of my outreach ministry and job as a staff chaplain with the veterans. Often, he, as well as some of the elders who were also veterans, would come to the VA Medical Center on Sundays to minister during our chapel worship service. When I was having trouble with my supervisor, my pastor sent some of the evangelists to pray with me and back me up in the spirit.

For about a month, they'd drive me up to Perry Point on Sundays and attend service with me to ensure I was ok. The prayers of the righteous prevailed, and things began to change and work out for my good at my job. I truly appreciated my pastor for sending me the help I needed at that point in my life.

To start my church transition, I set up an appointment to meet with my pastor to discuss my transition. I let him know that I was moving to Waldorf and praying for the holy spirit to lead me in finding a local church to join. However, my pastor didn't want me to leave. So, while I was praying for direction on a new church, he set up an agreement with one of the missionaries who lived near me in Waldorf to carpool with me to church on Sundays in Severn.

The missionary and I would meet at the nearby IHOP on Sunday morning and alternate driving to church. We talked and shared about the goodness of the Lord on our hour ride. The arrangement worked out for about a year. Then the missionary decided to move closer to the church in Severn. I tried to continue commuting every Sunday, but the 100 miles round trip in traffic got the best of me. After six months of driving to Severn by myself, I decided it was time to start visiting churches in my local community.

My former pastor from my home church in Silver Springs asked me to return there. However, that was still a long commute as it was an hour and fifteen minutes away from my home in Waldorf. Thus, it was the same situation as my church in Severn.

I was older now, and it was challenging for me to keep up with the aggressive speeding cars on the highway. I spent many of my younger years traveling around the Beltway back and forth to work and to see family and friends. However, I no longer had the patience or the desire to try and keep up that pace.

I visited a Baptist Church in my area for a couple of Sundays. Their services were very inspiring and encouraging. The pastor was anointed and spoke the Word of the Lord prophetically. I also visited a Church of God in Christ and attended their prayer service held Monday through Friday at noon. The prayer services were inspiring and helpful during my search for a church. After praying and seeking the Lord for divine guidance, I felt the Lord was leading me to join this branch of Zion.

I met with the pastor of the church, and we discussed my transition to their ministry and the possibility of me becoming an Evangelist at the church. While looking for a local assembly, I hadn't thought about the role I would be assigned on their ministerial staff. We agreed that I would take some time to pray and think the matter over.

Many of the duties I performed as a Chaplain were the same as a pastor at a local church. I administered Communion, performed baptisms, as well as preached and taught the gospel of Christ during daily services. Add to all of that my counseling certifications, and I could say I was more than qualified to serve in the role I was asked to consider. My only question was whether that was what God wanted me to do.

After praying and fasting, I humbly agreed to serve as an Evangelist. Before things were made official, I had to meet with the pastor, the Director of the Women's Ministry, the CEO, and the Elect Lady. During my interview, I shared my background and ministry experiences with them. I was well received and approved by the committee.

Naturally, there was an adjustment period. It was a different denomination, so a few things were not the same as my previous church. The pastor put me up to minister to the parishioners on multiple occasions. I joined the choir and started making new friends. Later, the pastor appointed me as a Mother on the Mother's Board.

Things seemed to be going great and moving forward until I hit a wall of boredom.

I told LaShawn, "Retirement is getting boring. I can't find enough to do with myself."

LaShawn said, "You know it's ok to rest, relax, and do nothing for a while? Enjoy not having to go to work every day."

I replied, "It's hard for me to relax. After working for 46 years, it just doesn't feel right waking up with no set schedule and nowhere to go."

I knew LaShawn was right. She hadn't said anything that my counselor hadn't already told me at some point. So, I took my boredom to God in prayer, asking him what to do with all the time I had on my hands. The Lord was faithful and started giving me directions.

At the prompting of the Holy Spirit, I began taking classes to recertify as a Substance Abuse Counselor, which required forty hours of continuing education credits. In addition, I started going daily to noonday prayer at my new church, which helped me refocus on my life goals. I also kept a daily journal to express my gratitude and feelings.

I realized there were so many things I wanted to do. I wanted to have fun, travel, exercise, bowl, write, and sing. But, most of all, I wanted to fulfill the calling of God on my life as I continued to pray and study God's Word. So, I continued to pray and ask the Lord for Divine Direction in this season of retirement.

I stood on scriptures like Psalm 57:2, which reads, "I will cry unto God most high; unto God that performs all things for me," and Proverb 3:5-6 which read, "Trust in the Lord with all your heart; and lean not unto your own understanding. In all your ways, acknowledge him, and he shall direct your path."

Trying to discover life's purpose can be stressful and overwhelming at times, but standing on these two scriptures helped me discover God's purpose for my life in that season.

Once I completed my recertification, I updated my resume and started looking for part-time work as a counselor. I went on several interviews, but all of the employers wanted a full-time counselor. Disappointed, I went back to the Lord in prayer.

The Lord answered me with the reassurance of his promise in Philippians 4:19, which reads, "But my God shall supply all your need according to his riches in glory by Christ Jesus."

I corrected my posture and leaned even more on the Lord for my daily directions. I set up a place and time to be with the Lord daily and minimized distractions during this time.

Each morning when I woke up, I asked the Lord, "What would you have me do this day? Lord, please order my steps in your word."

I then spent time reading the Word of God and meditating on it. I journaled everything the Lord placed in my spirit concerning the illumination and application of the scriptures I read. The more I spent quality time with God, the more my hunger and thirst for a deeper relationship with him grew.

The Lord showed me that quality time with him meant that I was to:

- Spend time in the secret place (Matthew 6:6)
- Pray in the early morning (Mark 1:35)
- Pour out my heart before God (Lamentations 2:19)
- Read and meditate on His Word day and night (Joshua 1:8)
- Be filled with the Holy Spirit and keep a praise in my heart (Ephesians 5:19)
- Always give thanks (I Thessalonians 5:18)
- and Write down what I received from the Lord.

As I focused on having a deeper relationship with God, I was led back to my passion as an intercessor. The prayer services held at my church daily at noon were uplifting during this time. Praying and interceding for others brought happiness to me and an increased sense of purpose.

The Lord sent one of the other mothers of the church to encourage my soul.

During our conversations, she often said, "Accept what God allows in this season of your life."

It was a simple statement, but the more I heard it, the more it encouraged my soul. I am so grateful for those words of wisdom. As I began to embrace and accept what God allowed, new doors began opening for me to preach and teach the word of God, one of which was a volunteer Chaplain position at a local hospital. In all things, the Lord was faithful in showing me that my joy was rooted in Him and that if I trusted His process, I would have everything I needed.

Chapter Fourteen

A s I continued to embrace retirement life, a major crisis hit the world. One day while in prayer, the Lord gave me a word that something big was about to happen. The world entered a global pandemic shortly after receiving this word. COVID-19 took the world by storm, and many perished. Countries across the globe enforced lockdowns, and here in the United States, almost every state entered into a state of emergency.

During the lockdown, all non-essential businesses closed, and people could only leave their homes for essential needs like food and medicine. Basic foods and supplies such as cleaning supplies, toilet paper, and medications were scarce. We were strongly discouraged from visiting loved ones to help prevent the spread of the virus. It was a lonely time as many were quarantined for fear of catching COVID and dying.

The constant news headlines about the number of deaths and positive test results sparked mass fear, anxiety, and depression. Then, as if the pandemic wasn't enough, the rise in unemployment, homelessness, violence, police brutality, and exposed racism added even more fuel to the fire.

I asked the Lord, "Lord, why are all these things happening?"

The Lord took me to his word and reminded me that these things must first come to pass, but the end is not yet. (Luke 21:8-12). The Lord showed me that COVID was a plague that He sent to get the world's attention. The world's system has taken God out of everything. However, it is time for that to change and for the hearts of men to return to the Father. The scriptures have warned us, so we must take heed and get it right with our Father in heaven. When God warns us, He expects us to change.

Understanding what the Lord had shown me about what was happening, I battled to stay free of depression and worry by spending a lot of time praying and seeking God's face, mercy, and covering. But I must tell the truth. It wasn't easy.

Not being able to see my family and friends took a toll on me mentally. Feelings of loneliness and abandonment began to creep back up. The isolation was wearing on me. At times it caused me to have feelings of anger and irritability, restless nights, and pains in various places throughout my body from stress and anxiety. I was frustrated because I could not change my situation or achieve the things I desired to happen in my life. Everything was on hold and out of my control.

I realized that I had to learn how to deal with these toxic emotions before they ruined my life. So, in addition to constantly communing with God through prayer and His Word, I found additional relief through physical activity, breathing exercises, and Zoom connections with my friends and family. All of which improved my nightly rest and sleep.

LaShawn once asked me, "Mom, how did you learn to trust God during these perilous times?"

I responded, "I learned that God is in control and He has the last say in everything that happens. Nothing can happen unless He allows it to be. So, I found comfort in His word."

We all face times of fear, anxiety, and stress. Below is the prescription God gave me in His Word to combat these times.

Philippians 4:6-7, "Be anxious for nothing, but in everything by prayer and supplication, with thanksgiving, let your requests be made known to God; and the peace of God, which surpasses all understanding, will guard your hearts and minds through Christ Jesus."

Matthew 6:31-34, "Therefore, do not worry, saying, 'What shall we eat?' or 'What shall we drink?' or 'What shall we wear?' For all these things the Gentiles seek. For your heavenly Father knows that you need all these things. But seek first the kingdom of God and His righteousness, and all these things shall be added to you. Therefore, do not worry about tomorrow, for tomorrow will worry about its own things. Sufficient for the day is its own trouble."

I Peter 5:7, "Casting all your care upon him; for he careth for you."

Deuteronomy 31:8, "The Lord himself goes before you and will be with you; he will never leave you nor forsake you. Do not be afraid; do not be discouraged."

Isaiah 41:10, "Fear thou not; for I am with thee: be not dismayed; for I am thy God: I will strengthen thee; yea, I will help thee; yea, I will uphold thee with the right hand of my righteousness."

II Timothy 1:7, "For God has not given me a spirit of fear, but of power and of love and of a sound mind."

Once again, standing on the promises of God helped me get through this tough time of transition in my life. God brought good things out of the heart of the calamity in my life. During the pandemic, I became more sensitive to the needs of others as I drew closer to God in my time of solitude.

As we slowly began to come out of isolation, I witnessed family relationships being restored and people becoming more aware and helpful with the needs of others. This time of transition taught me that we must trust and obey the voice of the Lord. Only through God can we stand firm and maintain hope and trust in His word while we wait on His word to perform in His timing.

The Lord made it clear that things would be different going forward. The pandemic was ending, but there was much work to be done. The Spirit of the Lord began to help me establish new goals and aspirations for this season of my life. God made it clear that in this season, I was to intercede for the Body of Christ, those who were lost or going through difficult times, and for our Nation and leaders. He also said that I was to write several books and then gave me the titles for each one.

I understood that no matter what I was going through, it was imperative that I completely surrender my life to the Lord. What God was asking of me was bigger than me. However, I began to seize the moment, trusting in the Lord with all of my heart and acknowledging Him in all my ways, knowing that he would direct my path (Proverbs 3:5-6). I asked the Lord to increase my faith and to help me in my unbelief and moments of doubt.

My faith began to increase even more as I continued to study and meditate on the Word of God day and night. The Lord gave me fresh wisdom, understanding, and knowledge of His Word. As I applied it to my life, it brought about a transformation in my life and heart posture. I denied myself and put God first in every area of my life, submitting to the will of God in humility. Then the shift came that changed my life. I received a renewed mind and faith.

AT THE PROMPTING of the Lord, I began working on the first book He instructed me to write. As I started the process of writing, I quickly realized that I needed a coach. I checked out several self-publishing companies and picked the one I thought was the best fit. I was very encouraged and inspired after speaking with one of the student success representatives and decided to join the Self-Publishing School in North Carolina.

The mind mapping, outlining, coaching, group sessions, writing rooms, and rough draft assistance were a great help in the beginning stages of writing the book. Then all of a sudden, I was hit with the warfare of health challenges. Unfortunately, this caused a setback in writing the book. I became discouraged, had no motivation or inspiration, and wrestled with writer's block for at least a month and a half.

The first health challenge was a blood clot in my right leg. As my first line of defense, I took the matter to my heavenly Father in prayer and fasting. Then my doctor administered medication and a procedure that dissolved the blood clot. I blessed the Lord for my healing and planned to press forward in my assignment of writing my book. But then, I encountered another health issue.

For several weeks I experienced unexplained dizziness and drowsiness. It eventually got to the point that I had to visit the local urgent care facility. The doctor said I was experiencing a side effect from the eye drops I had been taking for high pressure in my eyes. They then suggested that I follow up with my primary care doctor.

When I went to my primary doctor, they ran additional tests and found that my potassium was low. The pieces of this puzzle were coming together, and with the proper medications, I began to see my health improve. I blessed the Lord for the doctors, medication, and answered prayers.

Unfortunately, just as I prepared to return to my assignment of writing my book, yet another health challenge emerged. I started experiencing stiffness in my knees, which was often sore and painful. After going to the orthopedist, he prescribed physical therapy for six weeks. During physical therapy, I was given exercises to do daily and instructed to walk as much as possible. My body was working on healing, but my spirit was discouraged.

I became extremely upset with myself and the hindrance in writing my book. I prayed and asked God for understanding and awareness of what was really keeping me from continuing to write. The answer surprised me. I found out that I was my worst enemy. I was allowing some of the pains, wounds, and trauma suffered in previous years to prevent me from writing and moving forward.

Immediately I began to pray and seek the Lord for divine healing and restoration so I could continue writing the book as He instructed. To my avail, I was healed, restored, and refreshed to continue to work on my book. I was thankful to God and my prayer partners, coach, and family members who supported me during these difficult days in my life. With their love and support, I continued to stand on the promise of God that I can do all things through Christ, which strengthens me, and I continued to be obedient to God and write.

Chapter Fifteen

There are so many people, especially Christians, who miss God's instructions while in their seasons of transition, and I am not excluded. Looking back over my life, God showed me seven ways that I and many others miss him during the seasonal transitions in our lives. I am going to share them with you in the hopes that you won't make the same mistakes.

The first way we miss God in our transition is through sin and disobedience. I remember there were times when I prayed and asked the Lord for guidance and directions. Then he would give me the answer, but because it was not what I wanted to do, I did the opposite.

James 4:17 reads, "So whoever knows the right thing to do and fails to do it, for him it is sin."

So my disobedience led me to sin. Although it sounds terrible, I intentionally didn't listen to the voice of the Lord. I, therefore, was rebellious against him, even to the point of hardening my heart to his directions. I then had to live out the consequences of my disobedience. At times it was in the form of financial problems, and other times it was through afflictions and suffering in my body.

Only through totally surrendering my will in exchange for God's perfect will was I able to avoid this offense going forward. It was my priority to do exactly what the Lord instructed me to do, when He instructed me to, and how He said to do so. No, it hasn't always been easy or comfortable, but I moved forward, trusting the Father every step of the way.

Fear and lack of faith are the second way we miss God in our transition. Several times I lost faith in God because I did not trust or believe what He promised He would do in my life. I doubted His Word because it did not manifest in "my time" nor how I expected it to turn out. Having a microwave or genie expectation of our sovereign God will always make us miss what He is doing in our lives.

Then there were times when fear of the unknown left me paralyzed and unwilling to make necessary moves as the Lord had instructed, which resulted in my blessings being held up or forfeited. What most people fail to realize is that fear causes us to lack faith in God's ability to do what He said.

However, II Timothy 1:6 reminds us, "For God hath not given us the spirit of fear; but of power, and of love, and of a sound mind."

Unlike faith and prayer, fear and faith do not work together. Faith and prayer are twins that work together hand and hand. Prayer brings you to the door, and faith is the key that unlocks it. Faith encourages God's hand to move.

When I increased my faith through reading, hearing, and applying the Word of God to my life, a transformation took place first within me and then in other areas of my life. As II Corinthians 5:7 instructed, I learned to walk by faith and not by what I saw daily.

Impatience with God's timing is the third way we miss God in our transition. The Bible tells us to pray without ceasing (I Thessalonians 5:17). Well, I prayed, fasted, and sought the Lord about a lot of things, but nothing happened. As a result, I began to entertain a give-up spirit and, in some cases, took matters into my own hands. This, at times, got me into a lot of trouble with the Lord.

I was missing two important commands that went along with praying without ceasing.

The first can be found in Luke 18:1, which reads, "Men ought always to pray, and not to faint."

Then the second is in Psalms 27:14, which reads, "Wait on the LORD: Be of good courage, and he shall strengthen thine heart: wait, I say on the LORD."

It behooves us to wait patiently on the Lord as he arranges and rearranges things in our lives to bring about our blessings and needs. We cannot hurry God. He knows the time and season to bless us, and regardless of how it may seem, He is an on-time God.

Distractions are the fourth way we miss God in our transition. Everyday life is full of opportunities to do God's will, but we often miss them because we are distracted. We're distracted by money matters, material things, cell phones, TV, and so much more. As believers, we believe that God is the captain of our ship. However, when we take our eyes off God and put them on everything happening in the world around us, we lose sight of our captain. A ship without the proper captain leads you to adversities, sin, missed opportunities, and missed blessings.

When I became distracted and began following the crowd instead of being led by the Spirit of the Lord, I got into trouble with God. The noise of the world was loud, and it kept me from hearing the voice of the Lord. I allowed the many voices around me, with their thoughts and opinions, to be louder than the voice of my Heavenly Father.

John 10:27 reads, "My sheep hear my voice, and I know them, and they follow me."

Although I heard the Lord, I did not always follow. I hindered myself from moving forward because I focused more on what others wanted me to do rather than what God told me to do. To change this, I had to be bold, learn to say no, and then affirm that I am about my Father's business.

Don't be fooled. Just saying no wasn't always easy. Some parts of me still wanted to go along to get along. So, I had to spend time in the Father's presence, fasting and consecrating myself to realign with God's will for my life. As I intentionally turned down food and other worldly distractions, I rededicated my heart, mind, and body to God, surrendering my will to him. As I realigned, God did wonders in my life.

Disconnecting from God and the body of Christ is the fifth way we miss God in our transition. When I grappled with unemployment, Joe's abusiveness, and lingering pain from my birth mother, I withdrew from the fellowship of family, friends, and church. In doing so, I fell right into the enemy's trap of isolation. When you are isolated, all you have time to do is think and concentrate on what hurts you. I fell into a deep depression and wasn't sure if I'd ever see my way out.

Praise be to God! I found my way out with a little help from God and his Earthly angels. When we disconnect from daily prayer, studying God's Word, and fellowshipping with the saints, we become stagnant and distant from our true source of life.

John 15:7 tells us, "If ye abide in me, and my words abide in you, ye shall ask what ye will, and it shall be done unto you."

No matter what it looks like, we are to stay connected to God our Father through prayer, meditating on His Word, surrendering and obeying Him, and fellowshipping with the saints regularly. When we stay connected, we receive the comfort of the Holy Spirit and the backing of God as we navigate life's turbulent times.

Harboring unforgiveness is the sixth way that we miss God during our transition. I've experienced many offenses that left me angry, hurt, bitter, and confused throughout my life. For a while, I wore my hurt on my sleeve. Then, eventually, I buried it in my heart where it remained out of sight, out of mind until something would happen to trigger that pain and hurt all over again, making it a deeper and fresher wound.

When I started attending counseling sessions, I learned how my unforgiveness toward my family and loved ones was negatively affecting me. Unforgiveness is like a disease. It comes in, and before you know it, it starts infecting multiple areas of your life. It infected my relationships with friends and family. The trapped and suppressed emotions I carried from unforgiveness promoted sickness and inflammation throughout my body. Most of all, it caused a stigma in my relationship with God.

Matthew 6:14 (NLT) says it like this, "For if you forgive other people when they sin against you, your heavenly Father will also forgive you."

In other words, if I don't forgive those who have offended me, then God will not forgive me for my offenses to Him. What I came to realize is that forgiving someone doesn't mean that I forget what they did. But it does mean that I am intentionally letting go of the hurt and pain associated with what happened. So then, I can be forgiven by God as well.

Finally, while we are forgiving others, we must also forgive ourselves. There were times when the very person that caused me to be hurt in the first place was me. I don't know about you, but it's a task battling the enemy within. You're always together, and the negative self-talk track is on repeat. But God.

Through counseling and washing my mind with God's Word, I found forgiveness for myself and all the mistakes I have made. Forgiving myself required effort, humility, compassion, and understanding. Forgiveness healed me and allowed me to move on with meaning and purpose.

Philippians 3:13-14 reads, "Brothers and sisters, I count not myself to have made it my own yet; but one thing I do: forgetting what lies behind and reaching forward to what lies ahead, I press toward the goal for the prize of the high calling of God in Christ Jesus."

Forgiveness gives us the freedom to let go of what hurt us so that we can grab hold of the abundant life the Lord has predestined for us with divine peace.

The last and biggest way we miss God in our transition is by not knowing or recognizing the voice of God. Every believer can hear Him. The problem is we often intellectualize and overthink what it means to hear His voice. When I didn't recognize the voice of God, I missed out on many clues, directions, and warnings, which oftentimes resulted in a setback.

If you are still unsure of God's voice in your life, here are five ways the Lord speaks to us.

1. God speaks to us through His Word as we read and study our Bibles. (II Timothy 3:16-17, Psalm 119-105). When we read the Bible, the God-breathed scriptures will speak to us

PATRICIA A. BELL

divinely, giving us instruction, comfort, and inspiration.

2. God speaks to us through dreams and visions. Therefore, you should always journal your dreams and be prayerful to understand when the Lord is speaking to you through them.

3. God speaks to us through a small still voice in our hearts (I Kings 19:11-13). Some may call it intuition or a gut feeling, but most often, for believers, it is the Lord speaking to you.

4. God speaks to us through His Spirit during prayer (Romans 8:26-27). When you pray, you should always take a moment to sit quietly and listen for the Lord's response. It may be a scripture, a song, or a specific download or thought that comes to mind as you wait. That's God speaking to you.

5. God speaks to us through the confirmation of His Word by two or three witnesses (II Corinthians 13:1). When the Lord speaks, he most always confirms what he has spoken to you. Sometimes it's through prophetic words, something you read, or a word of encouragement from someone unaware of what God spoke to you.

Regardless of the specific way God speaks to you, we must learn the voice of God in our lives so that we do not

134

miss His vital instructions during our transitions throughout life.

If you find that you have missed God, simply repent with your whole heart and turn away from the things that caused you to offend the Lord. Remember, God isn't asking us to be perfect. He just asks that we trust and obey Him.

Chapter Sixteen

The Bible states in Ecclesiastes 3:1-8, "To everything there is a season, and a time to every purpose under the heaven: a time to be born, and a time to die; a time to plant, and a time to pluck up that which is planted; a time to kill, and a time to heal; a time to break down, and a time to build up; a time to weep, and a time to laugh; a time to mourn, and a time to dance; a time to cast away stones, and a time to gather stones together; a time to embrace, and a time to refrain from embracing; a time to get, and a time to lose; a time to keep, and a time to cast away; a time to rend, and a time to sew; a time to keep silence, and a time to speak; a time to love, and a time to hate; a time of war, and a time of peace."

In life, we all face transitional periods. For some, we may experience joy and excitement; for others, we may experience sadness, stress, and even depression. What we often don't realize is how we respond to these moments affects our outlook on life, our relationship with God, and how we interact with the people around us.

Simply put, transition means change. Change signifies that there is something to leave behind and something to move forward to. The Hebrew word for transition is MA'AVAR, which means to cross over or to pass through. Understanding the meaning of transition gave me hope because it reminded me that whatever I am facing is temporary, and I am only passing through that moment in time.

When transition comes in our lives, we do not always see the way forward clearly, which causes our faith and trust in God to be tested. It takes courage to let go of the past to embrace the new things God is doing. Appointed by God, seasons of transition lead to transformation, which is the key to us fulfilling our destiny.

For many years, I carried unresolved feelings, unforgiveness, and anger toward the people who hurt me in the past. If I'm honest, I even had some bitter residue toward a few of the hard transitions in my life. It was not until I wrote this book that I realized what was hidden in my heart. Many days, I cried and asked the Lord to heal me and give me a clean heart and a pleasing and acceptable spirit within me. Then, as the Holy Spirit brought things back to my remembrance, I forgave all who had hurt me, including myself.

After I suffered a while, the Lord gave me the scripture, I Peter 5:10, to meditate on.

It reads, "But may the God of all grace, who called us to His eternal glory by Christ Jesus, after you have suffered a while, perfect, establish, strengthen, and settle you."

Through transitions of adoption, marriage, divorce, unemployment, death of loved ones, retirement, and relocation, I had to find rest, knowing that my suffering was meant to transform and prove me in God. These moments in time were a part of the refiner's fire meant to produce spiritual fruit in me. The Lord gave me power when I was weak and strength when I felt powerless. Through Him, I was able to endure hardship like a good soldier in the army of the Lord.

Once the Lord settled me, my challenges were over. My mouth was filled with laughter and new songs. I learned obedience through the things I suffered. My Lord molded and shaped me into the woman He desired me to be.

The Lord elevated me to a place spiritually where my walk with Him could not be shaken. The testing of my faith made me stronger and built character rooted in the teachings of Jesus Christ within me. Casting all my cares upon God, I learned to totally lean on the Lord, knowing that His promises are yes and amen IF I obey his commands.

That wasn't the only thing I learned, though.

No matter what we go through in life, good or bad, God wastes nothing. Each trial, tribulation, and transition I experienced in life taught me a principle to build upon for the next stage that was to come in my life. Here are the nuggets of wisdom I learned along the way.

1. Transition is an invitation to intimacy with God (Revelation 3:20). During this time, He invites us to private time and conversation to look upon His face and know Him as never before.

2. Transition is not a place to get stuck. Instead, it is a place of release and preparation for the new thing God is doing. As we transition to our new season, we should take note of the lessons learned in the last season and release people, places, and things God has instructed us not to carry forward. (Isaiah 43:18-19)

3. While in transition, your mindset affects how it will be perceived. Therefore, we should stay focused on the good promises of God. (Philippians 4:8)

4. Detours and delays do not mean denial. All things work together for our good. (Romans 8:28)

5. When we surrender to the will of the Father, that's when unexpected miracles happen. (Mark 10:27)

6. As we lean on God in our transition, His grace will carry us through. (II Corinthians 12:9)

7. A season of abundance and an open heaven will follow if I am obedient to God's divine directions.

If you are in a time of transition right now, our Heavenly Father wants to encourage and empower you. He has you in the palm of His hand.

Isaiah 49:16 says, "See, I have engraved you on the palms of my hands; your walls are ever before me."

God is with you and for you. He knows the future and has already mapped out and lined up what needs to take place for you to reach your divine destination.

Thus, saith the Lord, "You are about to receive a delivery of God's heavenly supply for the new season and a fresh infilling of his Holy Spirit. If you don't seize the moment, you will miss out on your new opportunities. So go through the process, and be strong and steady about the work of the Lord (I Corinthians 15:58). I am going to reverse some situations in your life suddenly. You watch as well as pray and see me move by my Spirit. Don't let your left hand know what the right hand is doing. Something different is about to happen in your life. I am changing your circle. You will be found by the right person, in the right place, at the right time," Amen.

During times of transition, we must evaluate and seek God concerning the people and things that should move to the next season with us. If ever in doubt, the Lord will willingly clarify the steps you should take and the excess baggage you should release. Letting go of things that are past their season frees you up to grab hold of what God has waiting for you. So, go forward with God and be not afraid of the transition or the outcome.

Remember, change is a process and does not always happen quickly. But know God's timing is perfect. Little by little, step by step, the master craftsman transforms us into His beautiful masterpiece. So, wait patiently as the Lord stretches your faith and adjusts your alignment for your God-ordained destiny to unfold.

God's idea of success is different from ours. That's why it's imperative that we operate with a spirit of discernment and follow the Lord's divine instructions– trusting and obeying every word that proceeds out of His mouth. As we do so, we mature in God and experience a relationship with Him like never before.

Regardless of what I've been through in life, one thing I know is that I am a child of the Most High God. Getting to this place of peace and understanding wasn't easy. Some lessons I repeated more than once, but the more I trusted and obeyed God, the easier things got. The key was yielding to the Holy Spirit and totally surrendering my life to the Lord. Leaning on God allowed me to persevere through many trials and hard-ships that I thought would kill me.

Understand this. As long as we are alive, we will continue to experience transitions in our lives. I'm older and wiser now. So, with the wisdom I have gained, I will continue to seek the Lord with all my heart and harken to his every command. For as long as I follow God's voice, I will always be in position to thrive through life's transitions. I pray that this book has been a blessing and encouragement to you. Thank you for reading!

About the Author

Evangelist Patricia A. Bell is a retired Chaplain and native of Covington, Virginia. She transplanted to the Washington DC Metro area in her late teens. She obtained a Bachelor's in Business Administration from Strayer University, a Master's of Business and Public Administration from Southeastern University, and a Master's of Divinity from Howard School of Divinity.

Evangelist Bell has been in ministry for over 30 years. She received her ordination and endorsement from the National Baptist Convention and later became a licensed Evangelist in the Church of God in Christ. She is a board-certified professional counselor and a certified alcohol and drug counselor. She is anointed with a prophetic deliverance ministry and has a heart for winning souls for Christ.

Evangelist Bell's life experiences have taught her with God's word as a pillar of strength, nothing is impossible. Her favorite scripture of encouragement is Proverbs 3:5, which reads, "Trust in the Lord with all thine heart; and lean not unto thine own understanding." Currently, she ministers the Word of God throughout the DC Metropolitan area.